ASSESSMENT

A Teachers' Guide to the Issues

ASSESSMENT
A Teachers' Guide to the Issues

Caroline Gipps
Reader in Education
Institute of Education, University of London

Advisory Editor: Denis Lawton
Professor of Curriculum Studies,
Institute of Education, University of London

Hodder & Stoughton
LONDON SYDNEY AUCKLAND TORONTO

British Library Cataloguing in Publication Data
Gipps, Caroline
  Assessment: a teachers' guide to the issues.
  1. Students. Academic achievement. Assessment
  I. Title
  371.264

  ISBN 0 340 518499

First published 1990; third impression 1992

Typeset by Wearside Tradespools, Fulwell, Sunderland
Printed in Great Britain for Hodder and Stoughton Educational, a
division of Hodder and Stoughton Ltd, Mill Road, Dunton Green,
Sevenoaks, Kent by Athenaeum Press Ltd, Newcastle upon Tyne.

Contents

Acknowledgements

I should like to thank my colleagues on the Testing in Schools project: Harvey Goldstein, Bob Wood, Barry Steirer, Tessa Blackstone and Stephen Steadman who started me thinking about testing and its effects.

I am most grateful to Margaret Brown, Denis Lawton, Harvey Goldstein, Desmond Nuttall, Gordon Stobart and Gillian Sutherland who read the drafts for me; it is no reflection on them that I sometimes chose to ignore their advice. I must also thank Nicola Kennedy for word processing and Charles Knight for editing. Finally, many thanks to Marcus and Alexander who kept out of the way when things got hectic.

The publishers would like to thank the following for permission to reproduce material in this volume:
Constable and Co Ltd for the extract from *What Is and What Might Be* by E. Holmes (1911); Department of Education and Science for 'Improving the Basis for Awarding GCSE Grades', September 1987; HMSO for 'The IQ Question' Annex D from *The Swann Report* and the extract from *Primary Education in England: A Survey* by HMI; NCME for 'Measurement Driven Instruction: A Closer Look' by P. Airasian from *Educational Measurement: Issues and Practice*, Winter 1988; NFER-Nelson Publishing Company Ltd for 'An American View of British Accountability' from T. Bechel and S. Maclure (eds) *Accountability in Education*; The San Diego Union for the extract from *San Diego Union*, 12 December, 1982; SEC for the extract from *The Development of Grade-Related Criteria for the GCSE*, 1984; *The Times Educational Supplement* for the extract from 'Critics doubt results of code for fairer tests', 25 November, 1988; Times Newspapers Ltd for the extract by Donald Naismith from 'Putting Britain in the 'A' Stream', *Sunday Times*, 12 April, 1987; Trentham Books Ltd for 'The New Education Bill and Assessment – Some Implications for Black Children' by J. Eggleston from *Multicultural Teaching*, 6, 2, Spring; University of London

Institute of Education for 'The GCSE: some background' from C. Gipps (ed) *GCSE: an uncommon exam*, Bedford Way Papers, No. 29; Ward Lock Educational, East Grinstead for the extract from *Assessing Children's Language* by A. Stibbs.

Every effort has been made to trace and acknowledge ownership of copyright. The publishers will be glad to make suitable arrangements with any copyright holders whom it has not been possible to contact.

Introduction

This book is about assessment and the issues and implications surrounding its use. I am using assessment as a global term incorporating tests and examinations (whether oral, written or practical) and any other method of measuring children's learning.

Assessment has always been an important part of education and at formal and informal levels a part of every teacher's stock-in-trade. However, with the advent of a highly visible criterion-referenced model of national assessment all teachers need to have a far greater understanding of assessment and the issues surrounding it.

This book is written for teachers and others in education who want to know more about these issues. It is not a 'how-to' technical book, but a critical explanation which draws on the work of test developers, evaluators, sociologists, etc, and deals with the technical issues, where necessary, in as clear and comprehensive a way as possible. It is written for both primary and secondary teachers and deals with assessment up to age 16.

The fear of many teachers as I write this is that imposed assessment will come to dominate their teaching. Individual teachers have little real power to control or influence the path of current educational developments, but at least they can come to understand more fully the purposes, uses and limitations of assessment.

Caroline Gipps   November 1989

1

The Purposes of Assessment

Most books on assessment start by considering types of assessment: exams, standardised tests, graded assessment, etc, or the technical details. In this book, however, I am going to look first at purposes. I am going to ask, not what the assessment looks like, or how it works, but *why it is there*.

In order to understand why assessment of various sorts has come about it is best to take a historical approach. This perspective will also help us to set national curriculum assessment developments in context.

A brief history of examining

Formal qualifying exams for the professions began in Britain in the early nineteenth century. It was the medical profession which, in 1815, first instituted qualifying exams; these exams were to determine competence and therefore limited access to membership of the profession (Broadfoot, 1979). Written exams for solicitors came in 1835 and for accountants in 1880.

Why was it necessary for the professions to institute these qualifying exams? Part of the answer lay in the changing needs and structure of society. Before the nineteenth-century, England was a society in which social status and occupation were linked and determined largely by birth. Access to the professions was determined by family history and patronage, rather than by academic achievement or ability. As Eggleston (1984) points out, the celibate priesthood was virtually the only 'open' career opportunity in those times.

Soon after the beginning of the nineteenth century this static picture began to change. As the industrial capitalist economy flourished, there was an increasing need for trained, middle class workers. This need could not be satisfied by the traditional methods of nomination and patronage alone. The economy required, in particular, more individuals in the professions and in managerial positions. Society, therefore, needed to encourage a wider range of individuals to take on these roles. The expanding middle classes realised that education was a means of acquiring social status and they could see that it was in their children's interests to encourage them to aim for the professions. This was the first time that upward mobility became a practical proposition on a wide scale. Of course, there had to be some way of selecting those who were deemed suitable for training, as well as certificating those who were deemed to be competent. Thus it became necessary for the professions to control access and membership through examination. The examination was also seen as an important part of professionalisation.

The Universities were next: the demand for entry from the middle classes increased and in the 1850s Oxford and Cambridge set up Examining Boards and London and Durham introduced their own selective entry exams. It was still possible to buy your way into University, but before this, entry to University had been determined *solely* by family background. In 1855 the Civil Service entry exams were introduced in order to select candidates for the rapidly expanding civil service; though the aim was to *broaden* access, it was still almost exclusively those who had received an appropriate fee-paying education who were able to pass these exams (Eggleston, *op cit*). Before 1917 there was a range of competing school-leaving exams, some of which were linked to particular professions and Universities, but in 1917 formal examining at the end of secondary schooling was rationalised when the School Certificate was established. The School Certificate provided a standard school-leaving and university entrance qualification (Broadfoot, *op cit*), which was necessary because of the increasing numbers completing secondary schooling. To obtain the School Certificate required a pass in five or more academic subjects, with music and manual subjects being optional. The reason why the formal written examination of academic subjects was seen to be so important was that most of the early qualifying exams for entrance to the professions were written theoretical tests: because they were associated with high-status professions, this type of exam also became invested with high status. This then became the model for university entrance and School Certificate exams.

The point I am making here is that these examinations did *not* develop in a vacuum: examinations developed in response to the particular needs and requirements of the time.

The history of the development and use of intelligence testing, which played so central a role in schooling earlier this century, illustrates this point too.

A brief history of intelligence testing

The intelligence test movement developed originally as a separate strand from examinations. In 1905 Binet, a French psychologist, published the first intelligence test which was for identifying children with special educational needs. His approach to the development of the test was a practical, even pragmatic, one: items of an educational nature were chosen for their effectiveness in distinguishing between children who were judged by their teachers to be 'bright' or 'dull' (Wood, 1985).

At the same time, psychologists had been working on the theory of intelligence—trying to define 'the essence of intelligence'. In 1904, a year before Binet's test appeared, Charles Spearman published a classic paper on general intelligence. Binet and Spearman were critical of each others' work but the serendipitous timing of developments in the measurement *and* theory of intelligence gave IQ testing considerable appeal in the eyes of those responsible for the efficient functioning of the state education system (Thomson and Sharp, 1988).

One of the reasons for this interest in IQ testing was that as more and more children were brought into compulsory primary education, there was concern about the increasing numbers of children who were thought to be subnormal and therefore ineducable. Subnormality was, by the beginning of the century, seen as being distinct from lunacy, and such 'feebleminded' children needed to be sifted out from the rest of the child population so that they could go to special schools. Identifying these children accurately was clearly important: children who were not feebleminded should not be mis-identified, not only because of the stigma attached to going to special school, but also because the special schools were more expensive to run. Even at the beginning of the twentieth century, before the First World War, value for money was a prime requirement in education.

Binet's test was an ideal tool for identifying feebleminded children, and other group tests were later developed by English psychologists—notably Cyril Burt and Charles Spearman as well as by Godfrey Thomson later, at Moray House in Scotland.

Cyril Burt himself was installed in 1913 as the first psychologist for the London County Council to help with provision for subnormal children, and he used IQ tests to identify these children. Interestingly, Burt saw the definition of subnormality in administrative terms: 'mental deficiency must be treated as an *administrative* rather than as a psychological concept' (my emphasis) and 'For immediate practical purposes the only satisfactory definition of mental deficiency is a percentage definition based on the amount of existing accommodation' (Burt, 1921, p. 167). As the special schools of London could cater for only 1.5 per cent of the child population, this is where Burt advocated that the cut-off between normal and subnormal performance should be set. Burt found that 1.5 per cent of the population fell below a score equivalent to an IQ of 70 on the Stanford–Binet test (a modification of Binet's original test). So a cut-off of IQ 70 was advocated by Burt, to match the 'subnormal' population with the facilities then available to him. This IQ figure has been widely used as a cut-off point since that time.

In Burt's later book, he stated that he was not the only one to use an IQ of 70:

> 'Researches . . . elsewhere indicated that this average borderline [an IQ of about 70 per cent] corresponded with the general practice of the more experienced teachers and school medical officers, when nominating or certifying cases as in need of education at a special school; and, as it subsequently turned out, much the same standard was proposed or accepted by psychologists and doctors abroad. It was also adopted by the joint committee of the Board of Education and the Board of Control [in England] laying down standards for their investigator in their enquiry into mental deficiency.' (Burt, 1937, 1961 edition, p. 81).

However, considering Burt's reputation at the time, these others quite possibly took the figure from his 1921 book. Burt himself, however, seems to have forgotten how he reached the 70 figure, for on the next page he wrote:

> 'Accepting, then, a mental ratio [i.e. IQ] of 70, we have next to inquire how many children fall within the category thus defined. In London I found that the proportion of educable defectives was almost exactly 1.5 per cent of the total age-group.' (*op cit*, p. 82).

Which, of course, is hardly surprising, since that is why he chose the figure of 70 in the first place! I describe this in some detail because it is another example of an assessment being modified or used in a particular way, for a particular purpose.

The significance of Burt's appointment to the London County Council was that he was *not* a medical man: his post marked the beginning of the professionalisation of psychology as a discipline, with its own expertise and an aura of scientific respectability (Thomson and Sharp, *op cit*). These factors were crucial to the acceptance of IQ testing: it was scientific, and therefore 'objective', and the single figure was a marvellous shorthand way of describing children. This simplicity has always been part of the appeal of IQ testing. Furthermore, the theory behind the tests suggested that these measures could be used to predict future academic performance. As the focus in educational organisation shifted towards coping with the increasing numbers of children staying on into secondary education, so the role of IQ testing shifted from identifying children who were subnormal, to sorting and selecting normal children in the system.

An American psychologist, Louis Terman, had an important influence here. After Binet's death in 1911, his intelligence test was translated and revised by Terman. Terman was a firm believer in the influence of heredity on intelligence and was the populariser of intelligence testing in California and subsequently throughout the USA. He, like Binet, first used IQ tests to identify children with special educational needs, both subnormal and gifted. Terman's contribution to the debate was to suggest that pupils could be grouped according to their ability and follow different courses of study.

In England, the 1926 Hadow report on *The Education of the Adolescent* took this idea further. This report concluded that almost all children were eligible for secondary education, but not the same secondary education: it talked about the equal cultivation of different capacity. At the end of their primary school careers, at 11, children were to be classified by aptitude and to go to secondary grammar schools or secondary modern schools or remain in senior classes in the primary school. As the report put it: 'all go forward, though along different paths. Selection by differentiation takes the place of selection by elimination' (Sutherland, 1984). Again the intention was the most efficient use of educational resources and, where those resources were limited, that they be directed towards those children most able to profit from them.

These suggestions were refined in the Spens report of 1938 which proposed the (to us familiar) tri-partite division of secondary education in to grammar, modern and technical schools. The aim, however, was the same: 'all go forward, though along different paths' and the IQ test was to play an important role.

The Eleven-Plus: the need for selection

Clearly the concept of selection by differentiation required an assessment of the child's ability. Hadow, Spens, and the Inspectorate (HMI) suggested using examination papers in English and arithmetic and a standardised group intelligence test.[1] Local Education Authorities (LEAs) took varying lengths of time to adopt these assessment methods, some clinging to a system involving patronage and interview, but by 1938 what we think of as the eleven-plus was largely in place. When secondary education became free after the passing of the 1944 Education Act, the pressure on the selection process increased because access to grammar school was available for all.

There was another strand to the developing use of IQ tests though, and that was *equality* of opportunity. In 1920 Northumberland was the first LEA in England to use a group test of intelligence, and their reason for doing this was entirely egalitarian. The LEA covered both urban and rural areas and there was a tendency for schools in the more remote districts to submit few or no candidates for the scholarship exam to secondary school at age eleven. What the LEA wished to discover was whether this was due to a lack of ability on the part of the children, or a lack of resources on the part of the schools (Thomson and Sharp, *op cit*).

Equality of opportunity was also the theme in the period 1942–44, but this was usually interpreted as an extension of the Hadow principle: *differentiated* secondary education for all. In this sense equality meant preventing a wastage of talent. But, Thom (1986) points out, the Mass Observation Surveys found that the entrance procedures to secondary education were seen as one of the major *barriers* to equality. Instead it was suggested that intelligence tests and teachers' reports alone be used. This had already been suggested by R. H. Tawney as being more fair to all and a way of reducing the competitive struggle of the existing exams at age eleven. The White Paper of 1943 which outlined the 1944 legislation suggested that allocation to secondary school be by teacher report, with the aid of intelligence tests if necessary. However, Ernest Bevin complained that intelligence tests penalised the working class, while Cyril Burt claimed that selection *only* by intelligence test penalised the secondary schools, since children needed the right social background, as well as intelligence, to succeed there.

In the end, the 1944 Act did not actually prescribe the method of

---

[1] Sutherland (*op cit*) points out that in the interwar period the HMI would have liked to examine the entire age group, but the National Union of Teachers determinedly opposed this as it might be used to assess the work and effectiveness of individual primary schools.

selection, and it was up to the LEAs, therefore, to decide on their own procedures. Batteries of maths, English and IQ tests such as those produced by Moray House and the NFER were popular, especially since a battery was felt to be a better predictor of success at secondary school than a single test.

So we can see quite clearly that intelligence testing was linked with selecting and grouping children and was taken up in response to particular needs: first to identify subnormal children, and then to allocate normal children to secondary schools, whether on the principle of equality of opportunity or preventing wastage of talent.

Critiques of IQ testing and examinations

Although intelligence tests were seen by many as a tool of equality, there was also another argument. We have already seen how Ernest Bevin felt that IQ tests disadvantaged the working class. Sociologists such as Broadfoot would claim that intelligence testing was a means of social control 'unsurpassed in teaching the doomed majority that their failure was the result of their own inbuilt inadequacy' (Broadfoot, 1979, p. 44). Their argument is that intelligence testing obscures the perpetuation of class inequalities because it legitimates them. In other words, it was not that the middle classes were more intelligent, or better able to *acquire* intelligence, but that they *defined* it, according to their own characteristics or qualities.

Bourdieu and Passeron (1976) argue similarly that the middle classes, unable to perpetuate their status through capital alone at the beginning of this century, were able to fall back on a second line of defence: a school system which, though apparently allowing equal opportunity, was, in fact, geared to the culture of the ruling class and thus allowed them to perpetuate their privileged position by giving them a head start through success in the education system. Thus, we have the notion of 'cultural capital' as opposed to financial or material capital.

From about 1950 there was a reduction in the status of intelligence testing in both the USA and UK. This reflected a growing scepticism about the fallibility of IQ scores. In the USA this was due to the growing awareness that there was a 'cultural bias' in most tests in favour of children from white Anglo-Saxon backgrounds. In England and Wales it was the realisation that coaching and practice had significant effects on performance in the eleven-plus. On both sides of the Atlantic the importance of social and cultural factors in test performance began to be recognised and appreciated.

In England and Wales the need for selection and classification declined with the gradual move towards comprehensive schooling. IQ tests for normal children, in the guise of verbal reasoning and non-verbal reasoning tests, became largely unnecessary and thus the critique could be accepted without too much inconvenience. Equality of opportunity was now to mean that all would go forward to the same comprehensive secondary school.

There are sociological critiques of examinations too. The important point for our theme is that although exams, in particular public exams, are seen as an equaliser in education, the facts belie this argument. The distribution of examination success is persistently linked to social class, sex and race. Eggleston (1984) expands on the concept of 'sponsorship' in education, which suggests that certain young people are 'chosen' largely through their social background to compete for educational achievement. This concept is in opposition to the popular concept of open competition. For example, only the top 40 per cent of the ability band was thought suitable for GCE O-level, but this group contains a greater proportion of children from the higher social classes. So the competition for O-level was never truly open.

Again, Bourdieu's argument (very much simplified) is, that children from lower social groups are not less intelligent or less academically capable, but that children from middle class homes are better able to do well at school because of the correspondence of cultural factors between home and school. These factors include the sort of activities, books and language used, attitudes to reading and success at school, etc. Following the IQ argument, the sort of success that counts at school has been determined in terms of middle class values and experience. Thus, Eggleston points out, exams have a legitimating role, in that they allow the ruling classes to legitimate the power and prestige they already have.

Though individual children from non-middle class families do, of course, obtain academic success, the fact is that in percentage or statistical terms, it is a very much lower proportion than from more advantaged homes, and Bourdieu's argument is one way of understanding how this might happen. Here too, the point to be made is that there is more to be considered than the *nature* of assessment. The purpose of examinations, so the critique goes, is to maintain the social order as well as to select the competent. The anger of the extreme right Hillgate group about the change from O-level to GCSE and the accompanying change in what counts as important knowledge and skills, can be better understood against this background.

Recent developments

There has been a range of new developments in assessment over the last ten years, notably GCSE, graded assessment, profiles or records of achievement (RoA), as well as national curriculum assessment. We can extend the argument of this chapter and look at their *purpose*: again, these new forms of assessment have not come about in a vacuum.

The first three share a common purpose and that is to maintain the motivation of 14–16-year-olds, particularly those of lower ability in an era of increasing youth unemployment. GCSE and national assessment also have a curriculum control purpose. Of course, each development has other rationales and functions too—for example, to rationalise the 16+ public examining system for GCSE, and to revive a flagging interest in French for graded assessment. But here we will focus on motivation and curriculum control.

(i) *Motivation*

Examinations at secondary level are traditionally seen as having great motivating potential: they provide pupils with a powerful incentive to work just at the age when they are becoming resistant to parental and teacher control, and more interested in the outside world (Mortimore and Mortimore, 1984). Thus teachers and parents could, and did, appeal to the value of exams in the job market, and therefore, the pupils' own interests, as an incentive to behave well and work hard at school. As David Hargreaves has pointed out, this worked extremely well for many pupils (Hargreaves, 1982).

But, once there were very few jobs available for school leavers, and adolescents could see for themselves that a few qualifications could no longer guarantee employment, then the threat of exams was no longer sufficient to secure effort. Why should students continue to work at something in which they had little interest when the reward was taken away? Of course, here we are talking about *extrinsic* motivation, that is motivation external to the activity – doing something for a reward (e.g. to pass an exam or get higher grades) – rather than doing something because of the enjoyment of, or interest in, the activity itself, which is called *intrinsic* motivation.

Once it became obvious that teachers and parents could not use job success as a reason to work hard at school, other devices were sought. This happened with considerable speed (Hargreaves, 1988) because of the political and public perception of the threat envisaged by the trends in youth unemployment and pupil behaviour.

For example, early RoA schemes gave pupil motivation as a key factor in their development particularly for the less able, the group most affected by the failure of the work-hard-to-get-some-exams-and-therefore-a-job argument. The speed with which RoAs were taken up is evidenced by the fact that in 1982 and 1983 the Schools Council and HMI published surveys of early pilot developments (HMI, 1983; Balogh, 1982). But by 1984 the DES had produced a policy statement stating that *all* school leavers should have a RoA by the end of the decade. This is an extraordinarily rapid pace compared with most educational developments: it took 20 years to develop a joint 16+ exam. However, RoAs have now been eclipsed by national assessment.

The motivating properties of RoA are generally felt to include: recording experiences and achievements beyond the academic, thereby increasing the amount of success experienced by pupils, particularly the less academic; involving pupils in recording their own achievements thus increasing their self-awareness and independence; negotiating their assessments and future learning with teachers, thus encouraging them to feel that they have some control over their achievements and record; breaking up the curriculum into short units or modules with assessment at the end of each one because more immediate, achievable targets are more likely to retain enthusiasm than the long haul of public exams. Thus both extrinsic and intrinsic motivation are being addressed. There are, however, criticisms of using RoA to motivate pupils in this way. These relate to the role of education in shaping students' personal qualities to those required by employers and the view that they are potentially a device for surveillance and control (Hargreaves, 1986).

Graded assessment schemes, which also are felt to have motivating potential, are often linked to hierarchically-ordered units of study; each of the units is assessed at the end, leading to a grade. The assessment or test is clearly linked to the content taught and aims to assess what students know rather than what they do not know; after completing each section or unit and getting the grade, the student goes on to the next section or unit; the student should not take the test or assessment until he or she is virtually certain to pass. It is the intended emphasis on success which is the key motivator in graded assessment and three factors contribute to this. First, the student has only to demonstrate what is required for any grade to achieve it, whereas in public exams traditionally the grade awarded depends partly on how well others do, since only a certain percentage is allowed to get each grade, (although GCSE is slowly moving away from this approach). Second, shorter units of work and assessment are thought to be more motivating for many students than, for example, the two-year public exam syllabus. Third, is the principle of only taking the assessment when ready to pass. Although this is often difficult to organise with a class of children progressing at different rates, it is crucial since clearly more, regular, assessment is only motivating if it brings success.

It is usually thought to be the case that some subjects are more suited to a graded assessment approach than others (e.g. maths, science and modern languages). However, national curriculum assessment is based on a graded assessment model and will draw in English, history and geography which have previously been regarded as unsuitable for graded assessment. The introduction of graded assessment schemes in modern languages is generally agreed to have improved motivation, though the reasons are complex. These include a change in teaching approach involving more oral work and less written grammar, and more enthusiastic teachers, as well as frequent positive reinforcement of success for students. Whether these motivational features would be so effective if children were following graded assessment schemes in *all* subjects, is another question. We will look at this in more detail in Chapter 7.

GCSE, too, has a feature which is intended to increase motivation, though it is often ignored in the literature on assessment and motivation, and that is '*positive achievement*'.

Positive achievement sprang from the idea that the GCSE exam should allow all candidates to show what they *could* do rather than to present many students with tasks which they were likely to fail. Positive achievement, linked to differentiation, became increasingly important in the rhetoric of GCSE. As the new exam became a reality, Sir Keith Joseph talked about, and the DES wrote about, pitching papers and questions at different levels of difficulty so allowing *all* pupils 'to show what they know, understand and can do' (DES, 1985). The Secondary Examinations Council stressed that assessment should be a positive experience for all rather than a dispiriting one for some, and therefore candidates should not be presented with tasks that were too difficult (SEC, 1985). If assessment was a positive experience, the argument went, motivation would be enhanced.

The claim that GCSE will increase extrinsic motivation through positive achievement is compelling, but needs to be carefully analysed, particularly in the light of differentiated exam papers (Gipps, 1987b). The national subject criteria for GCSE state that for maths, modern languages, physics, chemistry, biology, science and business studies, differentiation must be achieved by candidates sitting different papers leading to different grades. However, there is a limit on the grades which can be obtained on each of the differentiated papers, and this may harm motivation; these issues will be taken up in detail in Chapter 8.

Continuous assessment through coursework is also suggested as having motivating potential. However, teachers face a dilemma over how to deal with feedback to students whose grades in GCSE-equivalent terms would be low, and the long-term impact of such feedback on motivation to complete the GCSE course. The changes in content and teaching style accompanying GCSE are likely to affect intrinsic motivation too, and there is some preliminary evidence that this has happened (HMI, 1988).

I hope what this section has made clear is that the need to improve the motivation of 14–16 year olds was a driving force behind these major developments in the first part of the 1980s, and that the concern over de-motivated, lower ability adolescents accounted for the speed with which the developments were adopted.

(ii) *Control of the curriculum*

The GCSE had another major purpose, and that was to shape the curriculum at secondary school level. Although the secondary curriculum has long been heavily controlled by examinations, the Department of Education and Science (DES) itself did not have any control over the exams. One of the aims of the DES since the mid 1970s has been to gain control over what is taught in schools, as Denis Lawton's account clearly shows (Lawton, 1984). One of the major changes brought about with GCSE is that the syllabuses have to adhere to both general and subject-specific criteria. These criteria were developed by the Government-appointed Secondary Examinations Council (now the School Examinations and Assessment Council, SEAC). The examining boards must submit syllabuses to SEAC for approval, and so all GCSE syllabuses must now conform to centrally-determined guidelines.

However, this central curricular control has been extended by the national curriculum and its linked assessment. The national curriculum lays down in outline, rather than detail, what children from 5 to 16 must study. The assessment programme linked to it requires that children are assessed on the objectives, or statements of attainment, continuously by teacher assessment and at the end of four key stages by external assessment. These results must be reported at ages 7, 11, 14 (and 16 for students who are not taking GCSE). They must also be made publicly available – in aggregated form – at 11, 14 and 16 by class, age group and school.

The detailed national assessments will no doubt provide useful information about individual children for teachers and parents, but it is the requirement to publish results which imparts to the assessment its significance. The perception of significance is, and always has been, crucial to the impact of assessment. The Revised Code of 1863, the infamous system of payment-by-results, made a substantial portion of the government's grant to primary schools, and therefore teachers' pay, dependent upon the performance of each child aged seven and over in annual examinations in the three R's. These assessments were therefore highly significant for the teachers. Work on other subjects was not forbidden, but since it was not examined, it was effectively discouraged. The minimum of the examination requirements all too often became the maximum attempted by the school.

The grant system as such was dismantled in the course of the 1890s, but the rigidly mechanistic teaching styles and habits fostered by it took much longer to disappear (Sutherland, 1987). British primary schools are currently full of standardised tests which are seen as routine and useful rather than significant, and thus they have little impact on teaching or curriculum (Gipps *et al*, 1983). Twenty-five years ago, however, teaching in primary schools was dominated by the demands of a highly significant selection exam at eleven-plus.

This is what is called in the American literature 'high stakes' testing. Corbett and Wilson (1988), describing the effects of raising the stakes (i.e. making the testing more significant) in two State minimum-competency testing programmes, found that the teachers' aim became to improve the next set of test scores rather than some longer-term, more general goal of improving student learning. Regardless of the teachers' personal and professional opinions about the tests, the fact was that students had to pass and teachers felt responsible to ensure they did. It would take a very unprofessional teacher to ignore the demands of an important assessment for his or her students.

It seems, therefore, clear that one of the purposes of national assessment is to make sure that teachers teach the national curriculum. Teachers, in Britain and North America, have a fine history of resisting innovations that they do not like, or approve of, or feel are unmanageable. One certain way, however, of making sure that teachers teach particular content is to tie it to a significant assessment: it works with public exams (HMI, 1979), it worked with the eleven-plus, it worked in the 1860s with the Revised Code.

To sum up, the message of this first chapter is that every assessment has its purpose and that much assessment is more significant than we at first think. We tend to think of America as being the country of testing, and indeed, to quote an American: 'Standardised . . . exams have become our nation's cradle to grave arbiter of social mobility' (Weiss, 1987). But we would be being naive if we were to think that assessment was much less significant in Britain.

In the next chapter we will look at the uses that are made of assessment (as opposed to purpose or intention) and the limitations that accompany all forms of assessment.

2

Uses and Limitations of Assessment

In the previous chapter we looked at the *purpose* of assessment: why examinations, IQ tests and the like came to be developed. Now we are going to look at the *uses* of assessment results, before considering some of the limitations.

We will consider six uses here: screening, diagnosis, record keeping, feedback on performance, certification and selection, though there are obviously others.

Screening is the process of testing groups of children to identify individuals who are in need of special help. A screening assessment programme requires that all children of an age group are tested and that some system for follow-up is available. Screening is widely used at primary school level to identify children with special educational needs. In a study carried out in 1983, in the wake of the Warnock Report, we found that 71 per cent of all LEAs had a screening programme (Gipps *et al*, 1987) mostly at ages 7 and 8, usually involving reading tests. However, in very few cases was the test score *alone* used to refer children for special help. The screening test was used to make the first identification but referral took place only after consultation with the teacher so that the overall *assessment* was based on the screening test score *and* the teacher's judgement.

Diagnosis involves using tests to identify individual children's strengths and (more usually) weaknesses. Diagnosis is the stage that comes after screening, but of course it is not necessary for screening to have taken place first; more commonly teachers themselves identify the child about whom they have a concern and wish to know more. Detailed diagnostic testing or assessment is more likely to be done by an educational psychologist, specialist or advisory teacher.

Record-keeping. In a study we carried out in 1980 (Gipps *et al*, 1983) the most commonly given use of tests at both primary and secondary level was record-keeping. This study looked at the uses of *standardised* tests, that is, the reading, maths and verbal reasoning tests, etc, which schools and LEAs can buy from publishers. Record-keeping is, of course, part of the transfer process—that is, test scores and teacher assessments are put into the child's record and they help (or are intended to help) in the transfer process from infant to junior or primary to secondary school. In general, record-keeping is the most passive use of test results. Looking at findings from other research into teachers' use of test scores, our conclusion that this was the most common use is not surprising. Becher and colleagues (1980) found that, though many tests were introduced for diagnostic purposes, their results were rarely used in this way. Teachers welcome the occasional individual check on their judgement but seldom find that standardised test scores provide new information about pupils or useful ideas for classroom strategies. Moreover, they found teachers were reluctant to make detailed analyses of test results, as these do not form an integral part of their teaching programme. Work in the USA (e.g. Salmon-Cox, 1981; Yeh, 1978) and Ireland (Kellaghan *et al*, 1982) found that teachers rely primarily on their own judgement and observations to make assessments about children (and to assign them to groups) rather than test scores, and our findings did not alter this picture. One of the most interesting findings to come out of our interviews with teachers was their view that testing was useful *for others*. The teachers did little with standardised test results themselves but were happy to go on using them because they might provide useful information for someone else. This is what usually happens within schools to test results: they are put into record books or cards and passed on. Teachers on the whole make little use of standardised test scores for 'professional' purposes, e.g. planning work schemes.

When the range of tests is considered, it is perhaps not surprising that so little is done with the results. The most popular reading tests used at primary level then (Young's *Group Reading Test* by LEAs, and the Schonell *Graded Word Reading Test* by schools) provide little in the way of detailed information for the teacher. Given this state of affairs is it surprising that the major use of test scores is their insertion into the record books?

Why then do teachers do so much standardised testing if they make little professional use of the results? Not all of it is imposed on them by others. The most likely answer seems to be that standardised tests are used as a safety net, i.e. they are an 'objective', externally produced means of checking that a teacher's group of children are performing at about the right level. Teachers seek this reassurance partly for their own peace of mind and also in case of questions over standards—for which use results from teachers' own assessments would not carry anything like the same weight. One of the outcomes of national curriculum assessment is expected to be a rationalisation of assessment and testing procedures at primary level, which would be no bad thing.

Feedback on performance. Feedback can operate at a number of levels: results of individual children can provide feedback to the teacher about both the child's progress and the teacher's success. Results of classes or teaching groups can provide heads and managers with information about progress and success of teaching across the school. The LEA can collect and analyse the results of tests and public exams; they can use this information to monitor progress for all their schools. The DES also collects and analyses public exam results which enables them to keep an account of levels of performance, not of individual schools, but of LEAs. A similar collection and monitoring of national assessment results will also take place.

This feedback of results can of course be used to *evaluate* schools and teachers. This is a major issue and one which is the subject of Chapter 4.

Certification. Tests and exams can also be used to certificate, that is to provide a student with a qualification which signifies that he or she has reached a certain level of competence or knowledge. The assessment is the means whereby we ascertain whether the child has reached the necessary level and the qualification is often represented by a certificate. Whether it is a cycling proficiency test, a graded assessment in French, or a GCSE, the outcome, certification, is the same.

Selection is of course a classic role for assessment as we discussed in Chapter 1. Currently, assessment is used for selection to different institutions within the state education system at 18, with selection for further and higher education. But selection can also operate in a lesser way at 16: it is usually necessary to reach a particular grade in GCSE before being allowed to study that subject at A-level at tertiary or sixth form college. In a less overt way assessment can be used to select students *within* institutions, for example, to allocate them to streams, or sets.

Twenty years ago, selection at eleven for secondary school on the basis of tests was widespread. With open enrolment and increased competition among schools in the wake of the 1988 Education Reform Act, it may be that selection to secondary school on the basis of national curriculum assessment results comes to feature large.

These six uses can be classified as to whether they are, in broad terms, professional or managerial. By *professional*, I mean whether the assessment helps the teacher in the process of educating the child, while *managerial* means using test and assessment results to help manage the education system. Screening and diagnosis can be identified as mainly professional uses, certification and selection can be seen as mainly managerial uses, while record-keeping and feedback on performance can operate at both levels. It is important to remember that if the main beneficiary of assessment is the child, then professional uses are the more important. Certification and selection are artefacts of our social and educational system; they, and the assessments which support them, are *not* central to the teaching and learning of the individual child.

The relationship between use and impact

If we look at how various tests and assessments are used we can begin to get an insight into their impact and the interaction between assessment and the curriculum.

Table One shows what, in general terms, different types of assessments are used for. The types of assessment listed are:

Infant checklists: these are assessments of pre-reading or reading skills, number or mathematical development, and social skills. They are widely used at infant level and usually involve the teacher checking off skills and activities from a list as well as the child performing some tasks. Many checklists are developed locally in LEAs by groups of teachers rather than bought from publishers.

Standardised Tests: have already been touched on. They are published tests usually of reading, maths and verbal or non-verbal reasoning used mostly at primary level but also at the beginning of secondary schooling. It is standardised tests that made up the *eleven-plus exam*, sometimes together with an element of teacher report or assessment. Recent figures show that 15 per cent of LEAs still maintain some eleven-plus selection.

Teacher-made tests and assessments range from the very informal—for example, a quick check on children's recall of a lesson or story, to the formal—for example, school end-of-year-exams. The advantage of this sort of assessment is that it can be constructed specifically to fit the curriculum.

Graded assessment: as explained in Chapter 1, these are series of tests or assessments, each one covering a specified amount of knowledge up to a clearly defined level of skill or knowledge. In order to pass the assessment, or get the grades, the pupil has to demonstrate that he or she can do, or has learnt, what is specified. Pupils are expected to pass (a high pass rate and regular certification leading to good motivation) and therefore should be entered for the assessment only when the teacher thinks they are ready to pass. The most well known graded assessment schemes are in music, modern languages and maths. Graded assessment is taken up in detail in Chapter 7.

Public Exams include GCSE (previously CSE and O-level), AS, and A-level. Most readers will be familiar with public exams and Chapter 8 focusses on GCSE.

National curriculum assessment as all teachers will know now involves a combination of continuous teacher assessment and external tests to be given at 7, 11, 14 and (for non-GCSE subjects) 16.

Table One Types of Assessment and their Use

	Scr.	Diag.	R.K.	Feedback	Cert.	Selec.
Infant checklists	*	*	*	T,S		
Standardised tests	*	*	*	T,S LEA		
Eleven-plus				T,S		*
Teacher made tests and assessments		?	*	T		
Graded assessments			*	T,S LEA	*	
Public exams				T,S LEA DES	*	*
National assessment	?	?	*	T,S LEA DES	*	?

Key = T teacher   S school

Leaving aside national assessment for the moment we can look at Table One and pose two questions: which of these uses is the most *significant* for pupils and which type of assessment is the most *important* in children's lives?

The most likely answers to the first question will be selection and certification and to the second, public exams and the eleven-plus. If we then ask which of these assessments exerts more control over the education of pupils, the answer would have to be, again, public exams and the eleven-plus.

It is fairly certain that you can remember your own school days being dominated by one or the other of these exams. Their very significance and importance mean that, for the age group of pupils concerned, passing is crucial and therefore that *teaching* is geared almost exclusively towards passing those exams. Of course this is not surprising, since what teacher would not want to give his or her pupils the very best chance of passing such important exams? As the last chapter pointed out, history shows us that the more significant an assessment is for pupils (or as in Payment by Results, for the teacher or the school) the more likely it is to control the curriculum and to dominate teaching.

Turning to national assessment, the use of assessment to control or determine the curriculum is no longer an issue, since the curriculum is now specified. But the significance of the assessments will make sure that teachers teach the national curriculum. National assessment is likely to be highly significant for children, not only because of its likely use in certification and selection, but also because of the requirements to report and publish the results of groups of pupils and because the children's performance on the assessment is likely to determine their class of teaching group, even at primary level. All our experience of assessment tells us that an assessment as significant as this has the potential to come to dominate children's educational experience.

Limitations of assessment

So far we have considered assessment as unproblematic, except in the overall sense of its role in the social order.

The limitations of testing are as much to do with the role of human beings as the tests themselves. Limitations can result from shortcomings in any of the following stages in the production or use of a test:

– the designation of the curricular model of the area tested;
– question design, standardisation and selection;
– administration and marking;
– interpretation of the score.

There is scope for human error and intervention at every one of these stages.

The first problem arises when a decision is made about what is to be tested. Before developing a test, or exam, the developer must define the curriculum, syllabus or range of activities from which, or against which, the test items or exam questions are to be developed. This is a subjective rather than an objective decision. For example, Harold Rosen (1982) made a trenchant criticism of the model of English language which the Assessment of Performance Unit (APU) language monitoring team adopted as the basis for developing their language tests. Also, tests of reading which focus on reading single words aloud, or the cloze technique, are based on particular models of what reading involves, yet there is no consensus about which is the best model of the reading process.

National curriculum Standard Assessment Tasks (SATs) will be based on the curriculum model exemplified by the attainment targets, programmes of study and statements of attainment in the national curriculum. So at least the field of content against which SATs must be developed is specified: it is not the test development consortia's job to do this. This reduces the limitation in one sense, but it is not necessarily the case that the national curriculum models for English, maths, science, etc, are the best ones.

The next limitation is to do with how tests or exams are administered. A *standardised* test is one which must be given and marked in a specified, i.e. standard, way. Thus giving children of different ages different time limits, or introducing a break into a test, will jeopardise the 'standardised' nature of the tests and thus make any comparison using those 'standardised' test scores highly dubious. We know that teachers do both these things and give children credit for items they have got wrong on the grounds that the child *should* have got them right. Similarly with exams we are concerned that there is no cheating either by students or teachers. The reason for this is that if important decisions hinge on the students' results then we want all candidates to have an equally fair chance. This, of course, is based on a particular model of assessment which does not include dialogue between teacher and student. Dealing with this issue is likely to be a major task for the SAT developers.

We also have to consider, though, whether the assessment measures what it purports to measure; this is called the test's *validity*. For example, does a single score on a reading test fairly represent a pupil's attainment in all the skills of reading? There are a number of ways of looking at validity[1] but for teachers the most important aspect is *content validity* which means that the test should match as closely as possible the objectives of the teaching it is assessing. Another technical issue is that of *reliability* or, put simply, if the test were given on a number of occasions to the same child, or

[1] See Raban (1983) for a more detailed and very readable account.

was marked by different people, would we get the same score? This is important for teachers because it answers the question: would this pupil achieve the same score if the test had been taken yesterday instead of today? The greater the reliability of the test, the more closely the scores on the two days would coincide.

These are issues which have to be dealt with by those who develop assessments. The choice by a school or LEA of which test to use must be based partly on reliability and validity issues which are discussed in the test manuals. Reliability and validity are linked and both are important, but validity is more so. A test which measures highly reliably, but is not valid (that is, does not test what it is supposed to test) is of little use.[1]

Testing is subject to measurement error as well as other factors, such as the child not performing well on a particular day. Just because tests give us a score, we should never believe that they are infallible. For this reason test results should always be interpreted in conjunction with skilled teachers' judgements.

But interpretation of results has its problems. Once we have the score, what sense do we make of it? The following passage from Andrew Stibbs' excellent guide on assessing children's language (Stibbs, 1981) illustrates the issue with regard to tests which give a reading age. This may seem an old-fashioned sort of assessment to use as an example, but the point is a general one:

> '. . . suppose we have a reading age for our pupil and we are aware of the limits of its reliability, its validity, and its comparability with national norms, how are we going to use the result? Perhaps we have an earlier score on this test for this pupil. If the later score exceeds it by more than the increase of his chronological age since the last test, what shall we conclude from that? Perhaps the anomaly is within the range of error of the test. Perhaps it is because the earlier test was administered by a different teacher who interpreted the child's pronouncements in a different manner. Perhaps the pupil enjoyed the test more this time – especially if he remembered doing it before – and was less eager to escape anxiety by refusing each obstacle. Or perhaps we decide there really has been significant improvement in his ability to recognise and pronounce words, beyond that which the increase in his age would predict. Are we therefore going to neglect his reading and give more attention to those who have made less progress? Are we going to recommend harder books to him, with no further check on his ability to understand them?
>
> Suppose another pupil has improved less than we hoped. Is the poor progress to be explained as all that can be expected anyway from someone who scores below average in this test, or is it a danger

[1] See Deale (1975) for a more detailed discussion.

signal? If it is a case of the latter, what remedial action does it suggest to us? Does it tell us why the pupil is making poor progress, or what his special difficulties are? Suppose the pupil's score is actually lower than in a previous test. Do we therefore believe that his reading ability has declined, or do we mistrust the test procedure?' (Stibbs, 1981, pp. 5 and 6)

Clearly, interpreting test scores is not straight-forward.

Information from assessments is only partial information and that of course is a serious limitation. For example, at primary level, information about children's progress has traditionally been based on reading and maths, not only because these are seen as the core subjects but also because they are easier to test than other skills or subject areas, for example singing or the ability to work as a member of a group. Even within the subjects tested, information is usually partial since, for example, assessing practical skills is rare. GCSE, with its emphasis on oral and practical assessment, provides more complete information than has been possible in the past for those subjects assessed, while Records of Achievement have the potential to offer information about the sorts of skills and qualities that are not normally assessed. If the national assessment follows the GCSE pattern and covers more practical and oral skills, this should increase the amount and range of assessment information.

There are, also, some problems specific to traditional public exams, which can be considered under the general heading of limitations. Exams have always emphasised recall of factual knowledge with a heavy emphasis on memory and rote learning; they also do not assess beyond the cognitive domain; they may be inaccurate (due to marker fallibility); and may not be a true reflection of what a pupil can do (since performance is measured once on a single occasion). As pointed out in Chapter 1, public exams emphasise extrinsic motivation rather than the desire to learn for its own sake. There are also serious reservations about whether performance in public exams predicts the ability to do well at university or polytechnic, or relates to the skills and qualities employers require. Some of these criticisms have been addressed in the design of GCSE, but many of them remain.

This sort of argument has led to suggestions that assessment should record information about a much wider range of achievements, lead to meaningful descriptions of what pupils can do, and enhance motivation (Murphy, 1986a).

As well as limitations, there are dangers in testing too, the most obvious one being the effect on teaching. As has already been made clear, the more significant an assessment the more likely it is that teachers will concentrate on teaching what that assessment measures and not teach other untested skills and activities. This is known as *curriculum backwash* and it can be a force for the good, as well as harm. For example the introduction of GCSE has resulted in an increase in oral and practical work in secondary schools (HMI, 1988). The aim is that national curriculum assessment too will assess oral and practical work and this will encourage the teaching of it.

Another danger of assessment is labelling: test scores and exam passes can determine ways of thinking about children. There are two issues here: first that the scores may not be correct, and second that they can affect teachers' views about what children are capable of doing (i.e. labelling can set an unconscious limit on what children are perceived as being able to do).

Until now, test results were often not communicated to parents. In the survey we carried out in 1980, we found that while at least 79 per cent of LEAs required primary schools to test at various ages, only one encouraged schools to explain the results to parents. That will now change with national assessment, and a great deal of care will have to be taken in explaining results to parents in a form that is not meaningless or liable to misinterpretation. The level of understanding about assessment varies tremendously among teachers and many will need in-service training before they can discuss results confidently and accurately with parents.

Very different issues will arise from the requirement to publish the scores of individual classes and schools. The best way to explain the results to parents (and 'prospective' parents) will be face to face, at a meeting, where detailed explanations can be made of the assessments, the school's performance in relation to its neighbourhood and to the influence of social and familial factors on attainment. Not all parents would come to such a meeting, so written reports will have to be available too. National assessment proposals state that information about class and school results should be available to governors, providing authorities, and parents; if they are to be made more widely available it should be as part of a broader report on the work of the school as a whole. Wider publication could well lead to league tables in the local paper and one suspects that this will become common practice for primary as well as secondary school results.

Governors will need to address some basic questions, such as who should have access to information at which level, and how confidentiality of individual results can be guaranteed where necessary. Information about class results will, at primary level, relate directly to individual teachers and must therefore be handled carefully. If Miss A's class in school X has a higher percentage of low-scoring children than Mr B's in school Y, what are parents to make of this? Is Miss A not as good a teacher, or does school Y have a 'better' intake of children? Does school X usually have a good intake, but this year Miss A's class was not as good as usual? Did Miss A's class have a bad time the previous year (maternity leave resulting in two supply teachers) in which case the results under Miss A's care may represent really quite good progress? Given the catchment area of school Y, should Mr B's results have been better? Publishing school results is not a simple matter, nor is communicating them to parents.

There are many limitations, and some dangers in assessment. There are also a lot of uses, many of them valid. We are, in any case, in an education system which is wedded to assessments of one form or another, so we have no choice but to use them. But it is important to know and to understand the disadvantages so that we can make the best job possible of assessment, with our eyes open and to maximise its professional use for the children's benefit.

3

Can Testing Raise Standards?[1]

There is often concern about 'standards' in education, though critics rarely say what they mean by 'standards', and evidence for this concern is usually anecdotal. Testing or examinations are then suggested as a way of raising 'standards'. In this chapter I want to look at what we mean by 'standards' in education, to look at how testing is used to measure 'standards' and consider whether, or how, testing can raise 'standards'.

The first thing to say is that concern over standards is not the prerogative of the 1980s and 90s. Both the Bullock Report (DES, 1975) and the Cockroft Report (DES, 1982) quoted complaints about standards in reading and maths from 60 and 100 years ago respectively. In the USA, standardised examinations were being used to *maintain* standards in the 1840s (Resnick, 1980). The interesting thing, of course, is the way standards are nearly always thought to be falling. Public concern over standards comes in waves and is often triggered off by activities outside the world of the classroom. When a cause for poor economic or technological performance is sought, the school system is an easy target.

For example, in America the demand for minimum competency testing (to set and therefore maintain 'standards') has come from parents, taxpayers and industry because of the rising cost of schooling, and high unemployment rates of school leavers, as well as reports of declining test scores among high school students. A similar scenario in the UK led to attempts to monitor national standards of performance via the setting up of the Assessment of Performance Unit in 1975, and to a national curriculum and assessment programme in 1989.

[1] Some of this material appears in B J Ed Studies, 36:1, 1988.

That standards are usually perceived to be falling rather than rising is referred to as 'the myth of the Golden Age' (Skilbeck, 1977): in thinking about the past, especially our own early lives, we strengthen our self-esteem by creating an idealised image of our experience. According to the argument, this image is threatened by change, particularly changes in education, thus schools will always be seen to be doing a poorer job than they used to. This explains why a single reading survey that suggests that levels of performance are not rising is more credible to the public than several that say that they are. 'The educational prospect seldom pleases . . . Certainly most people seem to feel they were helped by their educational experience, even those whose life chances would appear to have been impoverished by it' (MacDonald, 1978).

It is also the case that, since more young people are staying on at school than in the 1950s and 1960s, employers and parents who are concerned about standards of school leavers are probably comparing groups of different abilities, since when they were at school only the 'brighter' children stayed on.

What do we mean by standards?

'Standards' is a term which is probably more loosely used than any other in education. When we talk about standards we may be referring to levels of *attainment* in basic skills such as reading and maths, or levels of attainment in a much wider range of school activities; we may be talking about standards of *provision*, e.g., the number of teachers and books per child, or we may be talking about behaviour, dress and other *social phenomena*. So, in the narrowest sense, standards can mean levels of performance on a test, and in the widest sense can encompass notions of social and moral behaviour and discipline as well as educational attainment. It is when defined most widely, moving into the area of general values, that the term is most prone to subjective and anecdotal use. The link between the narrow and wide uses of the term is tenuous, but one that is often made. In the minds of the general public, a decline in standards of dress and 'moral' behaviour, which may well be due to changing social and cultural conventions, is likely to be linked with a perceived decline in educational standards. Educational standards however, are probably most often defined in terms of performance in the basic skills and are therefore related to test scores and exam results. There is without doubt an attraction in using these scores, so easily reduced to a single figure, as a form of shorthand in which to report performance in complex skills such as a language or maths.

There may be all sorts of caveats and contextual information to go alongside the scores but this is usually forgotten or discarded. As an American educator has put it:

> 'There is a strong tendency for quantitative data to overwhelm other forms of information. Test scores are easy to feature in newspaper headlines and they have an appeal difficult to resist. The complex interpretations of what the data mean do not have the same persuasion nor lend themselves to similar exploitation by the mass-media' (House, 1978).

The fact that many members of the public feel that educational standards are falling is one which we ignore at our peril. In the current climate, when consumerism is the dominating educational ideology (Lawton, 1987), parents', employers' and politicians' opinions about standards are vitally important. The view that standards are declining provides politicians with the impetus and rationale for the setting of approved standards (in the form of levels of test performance) in order to ensure quality control. An example of this was Sir Keith Joseph's objective for GCSE: to bring 80–90 per cent of all 16 year old pupils *at least* (his emphasis) up to the level associated with the grade of CSE which was achieved by average pupils. Now we have national curriculum attainment targets to set the standards throughout the years of schooling.

This argument is put clearly by Donald Naismith, Director of Education for Wandsworth:

> '. . . The establishment of standards, which must be consistent with international expectations, is a necessary condition for the restoration of the commitment to excellence missing from many parts of the education service. In the absence of external standards, pupils and teachers have no alternative but to establish their own. Understandably, these standards are all too often too low . . . Standards will make the education service truly accountable to parents . . . They will also provide the public with a means of measuring the effectiveness of the education system . . . Standards will enable administrators to target their budgets where improvements are needed, instead of, as now, in ways unrelated to any sense or expectation of educational performance: there is little point in comparing levels of expenditure – unit costs, pupil–teacher ratios or class sizes – if no one knows how effectively the money is used . . . The introduction of a national curriculum and universal standards would guarantee equality of opportunity to the pupil, accountability to parents and the public, intellectual rigour to the programme of learning, and enable the education service to be managed in ways which relate financial output to educational output . . .' (12 April 1987, *Sunday Times*)

Not only do his comments make the 'establishment of standards' seem immensely sensible, they bring up the difficult issue of how to get a measure of value for money for the taxpayer and accontability for parents within the educational system. Anathema though such ideas may have been to many professionals, these are issues which have come to the fore in the 1980s and 1990s. The question on the agenda is: How do we know that we are getting value for money unless we have some assessment of standards of performance? 'Standards' always come back in some way to pupil performance, which in turn is assessed by exams or tests.

The early discussions about the national curriculum assessment programme made it sound as though, public examinations apart, there was little testing within the system, and certainly that testing children at 7 and 11 would be a new development. This is simply not true: there was a considerable amount of testing going on in schools at 7, 9 *and* 11 and one of the major purposes of this testing was to monitor standards. There are two surveys which relate directly to this and I shall outline the findings to make the point.

In 1980 we carried out a survey (which I referred to briefly in the previous chapter) of all LEAs asking about any testing programmes they had, that is, standardised tests of reading, maths, etc, given routinely to all or part of an age group (Gipps *et al*, 1983). We discovered that testing was widespread, with at least 79 per cent of LEAs doing some kind of testing. This testing focused on the basic skills (reading, maths and English) together with verbal and non-verbal reasoning tests. Of these, reading was by far the most commonly tested skill, with the beginning and end of the junior school (7 and 11) being the most popular stages for this testing. Testing at 11+ was the most common and it is at this age that verbal reasoning tests were most used. But testing at 7 was widespread. There was some LEA-organised testing at secondary level, though much less, usually on entry to secondary school, or at 13 to help in option choice.

Towards the end of 1983 we sent another questionnaire to all LEAs, this time asking specifically about screening programmes, that is, tests or checklists given routinely to all or part of an age group with the purpose of identifying children with special educational needs (Gipps *et al*, 1987). Again, testing was widespread, with 71 per cent of all LEAs having at least one such programme. Although this might look like a relative decline in the level of testing since 1980 we cannot make this assumption, since in the two surveys we were asking about different things: in the second survey we were asking specifically about screening programmes. These tend to be used at younger ages and to involve reading tests exclusively. The most common ages for screening were 7 and 8.

So the evidence shows that, contrary to belief, there has been a great deal of testing in schools, particularly in the 7- and 8-year-old groups.

Monitoring standards of performance

In our earlier study we asked LEAs why they had these testing programmes and to what uses they were put. A total of 50 LEAs out of the 82 which replied gave monitoring of standards as one, or the sole, reason for their testing programmes. This involved both monitoring LEA-wide results, to compare them with national results, and monitoring of school results, which involves comparing schools. We also know from this survey that while LEAs use tests quite extensively to monitor standards in schools, they tend to use the results 'professionally', which means privately, rather than, for example, publishing league tables. Commonly each school will receive its own test scores together with those of the LEA as a whole or divisions within the LEA. There may be a visit from the adviser/inspector to discuss the school's results, or there may be discussion at a Heads' meeting. However, our research in schools showed the use of formal meetings to be infrequent.

By contrast, public exam results (GCSE and A-level) are analysed rather more publicly, particularly in the wake of the 1980 Education Act which requires schools to publish their results. The DES also analyses these exam results and comments on standards: the English School Leavers Survey – essentially a statistical analysis of exam results – says: 'Taken over the six years (1977/8 to 1983/4) the qualifications of school leavers have shown modest but steady improvement' (DES, 1986). However this is not proof that 'standards' are rising. Statistics of this kind are difficult to interpret because GCE grading largely was norm-referenced (when grades are awarded on the basis of how a student fares in comparison with other candidates) rather than criterion-referenced (where there is an attempt to compare a student's performance with some 'absolute' standard).

This is a useful point at which to consider norm- and criterion-referenced assessment. In norm-referenced assessments all the students' scores are put into a distribution table (or graph) and a certain percentage are assigned each grade (eg only 10 per cent will be awarded grade A, 20 per cent grade B and so on); or a cut-off point is chosen for passing, allowing a certain percentage to pass and the rest to fail. Clearly, the grade a student gets, or whether she or he passes or fails, depends partly on the performance of the other students. This came to be seen as unfair, particularly in the case of public exams, hence the shift to criterion-referencing in GCSE.

Standardised reading tests are a particular form of norm-referenced test. In the development, or standardisation, of a test the spread of scores achieved by a large sample of children of particular ages is used as a reference point. Subsequently when the test is given to a child, his or her score (called raw score) is compared with this table of scores to give a 'standardised' score which indicates where the child stands in relation to the scores of the original large sample and therefore whether the child is average, above or below compared with this reference group. Usually 100 is given as the average with a standard deviation of 15 which means that any *standardised score* from 85 to 115 is within the average range, i.e. 100 plus or minus 15. Thus if a raw score of 35 on a test converts to a standardised score of 120, then a child who scores 35 on the test is, according to that test, of above-average reading ability compared with other children of the same age.

A *reading age* is a particular form of standardisation conversion. If, in the standardisation of the test the average score for children of 8 years 6 months was 35, then a child who gets a raw score of 35 on that test would be said to have a reading age of 8 years 6 months regardless of his or her actual age.

Criterion-referenced assessments, on the other hand are designed to reflect whether or not a student can do a specific task, or range of tasks, rather than to measure how much better or worse his or her performance is in relation to that of other students. Thus levels or criteria of performance are set and the students are marked or graded according to whether they reach the level or attain the criterion. In this system there is no limit to how many students can reach any level: hence Sir Keith Joseph's aim of getting 80–90 per cent of 16 year olds up to the level previously deemed to be average. On norm-referenced tests there is no point in trying to get every pupil to achieve an average or above average score since, by definition, these tests are designed to have half the population scoring above and half below the mean.

Given this difference between the two sorts of assessment, we can see that norm-referenced assessment cannot tell us about changes in standards of performance over time. In the case of O-level, CSE and A-level, the *numbers* of candidates gaining any particular grade will fluctuate (depending on the numbers entering *and* their performance) in order to keep the *proportions* gaining each grade roughly constant from year to year. Since this is the case, the number of passes will increase automatically as the number of candidates rises (to keep the proportion of passes stable) even if the overall performance of candidates does not rise. The accusation that, for example, A-levels are wholly norm-referenced is vehemently denied by the senior examiners who play the key role of carriers of standards from year to year, but the norm-referenced structure militates against the measure of absolute standards. Will the GCSE be any better at telling us whether 'standards' are going up or down? It can only do that, of course, if it becomes a true criterion-referenced examination. Since the development of grade related criteria (the criteria which would make it criterion-referenced) is causing many problems at the moment (see Chapter 8), it seems a long way off.

National curriculum assessment is also proposed as a criterion-referenced assessment system. The statements of attainment are the criteria and children will have reached a level once they have 'passed' or attained the statements of attainment for that level. There will be no artificial limit on the number of children reaching each level and the numbers reaching each level will, over the years, be a guide to what is happening to standards of performance in the assessed part of the national curriculum. We do, of course, already have a national assessment programme which was set up with a brief to monitor standards. The Assessment of Performance Unit (APU) is a unit, until recently within the DES, which supervised the national assessment of performance in maths, language, science, modern languages and design technology. Although the APU was set up at a time of concern over the education of minority children and had as one of its tasks to identify underachievement, in reality its main task, as far as the DES was concerned, was to operate as an indicator of educational standards and to give ministers information on whether, and by how much, these were rising or falling (Gipps and Goldstein, 1983).

The APU made little progress on its task of providing information on standards and how these are changing,[1] because there is a major technical problem in measuring changes in performance on tests over time. Changes large enough to be meaningful will only be detected over a number of years – at least four or five – and any serious monitoring of performance would go on over a longer period than that. For example, the NFER national reading surveys ran from 1948 to 1972. The problem is that the same test used over that sort of period becomes dated. The curriculum changes, teaching changes, and society changes, affecting, for example, our use of language. So the test becomes harder and standards will seem to fall. To make the test 'fair' it is necessary to update it, but then you cannot compare the results on the modified version of the test with

---

[1] For a detailed critique of the standards issue in relation to national assessment programmes see Wood and Power (1984).

the results on the original form because it is not a true comparison. The same problem is true of exams: a Schools Council study of the feasibility of comparing standards of grades awarded in 1963 and 1973 in A-level English literature, mathematics and chemistry (basically by getting 1973 examiners to mark 1963 papers) concluded that changes in the syllabuses and methods of examining over the period made it impossible to draw conclusions about changes in standards (Christie and Forrest, 1980).

The problem the APU ran in to is that various statistical techniques can be used to calculate comparable difficulty levels and there is no consensus on which of them is satisfactory. In the early 1980s the APU had to drop the controversial Rasch technique of analysing difficulty levels of test items and admit that it could not comment on trends in performance over time, i.e., 'standards'. What it did do, however, was to use a pool of common items which it decided had not dated and looked at performance on those over a four year period of performance. This gave some guide to what is happening to levels of performance, but the pool of common items will, however, decrease over time. For example, what the maths work has shown is that, on these items, there has been a small but significant increase in the percentage of children passing at both 11 and 15 between 1978 and 1982 (Cambridge Institute of Education 1985). But this has been a very small and limited part of the APU's work.

While the APU can only make tentative comments about changes in levels of performance, their results can however be used to give hard facts about what children of 11 and 15 can do in certain subjects. For example, when the Chairman and Chief Executive of Jaguar Cars claimed that of the young people applying for apprenticeship a third 'couldn't even add up six plus nine', the Deputy Director of Education for Coventry responded by pointing out the findings of the APU. After all the APU had reported that 94 per cent of 15 year olds could add two *four-digit* figures (*TES*, 16.5.1986). The same article reported the Minister for Information Technology as saying 'Schools are turning out dangerously high quotas of illiterate, innumerate, delinquent unemployables'. The appraisal of the findings of the APU Language Team reported, however, that 'No evidence of widespread illiteracy was discovered. On the contrary the evidence is that most pupils have achieved a working literacy by the age of 11' and 'No collapse of standards was discovered. Over the five years of the surveys, improvement in the performance of primary pupils was evidenced, while secondary performance remained 'fairly static' (Thornton, 1986). There is, of course, always room for politicians to ignore the data if it does not suit them, and for educationalists to argue over its meaning.

To sum up this section, we have to conclude that, although there is a great deal of testing and examining in the school system, it can only provide us with limited information on standards of performance. This is for a number of reasons: at LEA testing level because of the limited number of subjects covered, and private/professional use of results; at public exam level because of the norm-referenced approach which does not permit measure of 'absolute' standards; at APU level because of the difficulties in analysing tests which have to change in content over extended periods of time.

However, the plan in national curriculum assessment is to use tests to *set*, and raise, standards rather than just to measure them. National curriculum assessment may be able to do a better job of providing information about standards; it is to be criterion-referenced and although the assessment material will change over time, if the levels and statements of attainment are kept the same it should be possible to compare the numbers of children at the different levels from one year to the next.

Using tests to set standards

The idea that tests can measure standards in education is one thing. The idea that testing can *raise* standards is quite another, yet this has received even less critical attention. The implicit belief is that introducing a testing programme will raise standards. The publication of exam results was seen as being one way of maintaining standards, an argument foreshadowed in a leaflet produced by the National Council of Educational Standards (Bogdanor, 1979). This essay suggested 17 ways of 'improving standards in our schools' including monitoring through tests, exams, and HMI full inspections, the results of which should all be made public. The connection between testing and improved performance is, however, rarely made explicit. The stimulus (testing) is applied and the outcome (improved test performance) hoped for, but the process linking the two remains vague and undisclosed. We do have some ideas, of course, about why (or rather how) introducing a testing programme will lead to a rise in test scores:

1. It can focus attention on the subject being tested and so more time is spent teaching that subject than previously.
2 It may result in teaching to the test, which is quite likely to result in improved performance on the test. However, if test results rise as a consequence of teaching to the test rather than as a consequence of some other change in the classroom process, is such a rise necessarily worth while?

3. Curriculum backwash may occur: that is, test content may have an impact on teacher practice other than teaching to the test. The received notion has been that backwash is bad, mostly on the grounds that tests concentrate on only a small part of the curriculum and the danger is that too much time can be spent in preparing for them. But it is also the case that, sometimes, tests can be used as an engine of covert curriculum reform in order to enrich the curriculum, and certainly some of the APU assessments seem to have had this effect.

The more significant the assessment, remembering Chapter 1, the more likely teaching to the test and curriculum backwash will be. A quote from an American newspaper nicely illustrates the effect:

> **'Teaching to Test' Credited with Improvements in Basic Skills.**
> Students in San Diego County public schools scored better this year on every phase of the state's annual battery of basic skills tests, especially in districts gearing their curriculum to fit the exams . . . The lesson many school districts have drawn . . . is that if a school system wants to score high it should 'teach to the test'. 'That doesn't mean they're cheating,' said Pierson (pupil services director) 'but they are moulding their curriculum to fit what the CAP tests.' (San Diego Union, 2 December, 1982, page B-1)

Will the national curriculum and assessment raise standards?

As we have seen, there is little evidence that the introduction of testing raises 'standards' short of teaching to the test. However, what we have in national curriculum assessment is the introduction of testing linked to specific curriculum objectives (the statements of attainment) and a high significance placed on the results. There is little doubt about the significance of national curriculum assessment results. Students are to be graded and classified; schools, and indeed some teachers, are to be evaluated on the basis of the results; if they are found wanting, schools may have to close and teachers may face redundancy, or lack of promotion. Even if a particular teacher's job is not on the line, nor the school unpopular, teachers will be conscious of the importance of the assessment results for children's life chances. The significance, therefore, will operate at every level.

The perception of significance is, as we have already said, crucial to the impact of assessment. In America highly significant testing is called 'high stakes' testing. Madaus (1988) has analysed the relationship between the level of stakes a test is perceived to have and the effects of the test, and come up with a number of hypotheses, the most relevant to our purposes being:

– the power of tests and examinations to affect individuals, institutions, curriculum or instruction is a perceptual phenomenon: if students, teachers, or administrators believe that the results of an examination are important, it matters very little whether this is really true or false—the effect is produced by what individuals *perceive* to be the case; and
– when test results are the sole or even partial arbiter of future educational or life choices, society tends to treat test results as the major goal of schooling rather than as a useful but fallible indicator of achievement.

Two other Americans, Corbett and Wilson (1988), describing the effects of actually raising the stakes in two state minimum competency testing (MCT) programmes, found support for these hypotheses, in particular that the aim becomes to improve the next set of test scores rather than some longer-term, more general goal of improving student learning. Regardless of the teachers' personal and professional opinions about the tests, the fact was that students had to pass and teachers felt responsible to ensure they did. It would take a very unprofessional teacher to ignore the demands of a life-controlling assessment for his or her students.

There is little doubt that our national curriculum assessment programme will be 'high stakes' but it is *not* to be a minimum competency programme. Again, turning to American writers, their prediction is that in what they call Measurement Driven Instruction, i.e. using 'high stakes' achievement tests to drive the teaching process, the greatest impact on instruction will occur, not in a MCT situation, but when both the test standards and stakes are high. That is, the influence on teaching is greatest when the consequences associated with test performance are important and when the standard for passing is challenging, yet attainable (Airasian, 1988). This looks very much like the situation in national assessment.

It does look as though standards of performance on the national assessments will rise as teachers become familiar with the curriculum and assessment arrangements and gear their teaching towards them. Under the new system with ultimately a wide range of subjects being assessed, if the curriculum is good and wide, and the assessments are educationally valid and enabling, will teaching to the test still be a cause for concern? Perhaps not, only time will tell. For now we can conclude that using imposed testing in conjunction with clear teaching objectives in a 'high stakes' setting, with high yet attainable standards is likely to succeed in raising standards of test performance. And of course the broadening of the curriculum, for example introducing science for infants, may be seen as part of improving 'standards' of education in general.

There are other issues to consider, however, such as the effects of increased competition on the less able, and these will be dealt with in the final chapter.

4

Assessment and Evaluation of Schools

National curriculum assessment results are going to be used to evaluate school performance. The publication of distributions of scores on national curriculum assessment at 11, 14 and 16 (for subjects which are not taken at GCSE), and possibly at 7, is seen as a novel way of monitoring school performance. But this is by no means the first attempt to develop an output measure of schools in recent years. The first of these attempts was via the APU.

In the previous chapter I described what happened to the APU's attempts to monitor changes in standards of performance over time. In this chapter I shall trace the various attempts to monitor and evaluate school performance through the analysis and publication of assessment results, including the APU's.

The Assessment of Performance Unit

In the growing atmosphere of accountability in the late 1970s, when it became clear that the APU was intending to monitor standards of performance, there was considerable concern that it was intending to focus on individual schools. If this was to be the case, the fear was that this national assessment programme would come to be used as an instrument to evaluate schools and therefore teachers.[1] Although the APU's assessment programme was to deal with *children*'s standards of performance, this was interpreted as potentially deal-

---

[1] A detailed evaluation of the APU can be found in Gipps and Goldstein (1983) and Gipps (1987a).

ing with teachers' performance. The teaching unions, therefore, viewed it with great concern. The idea of teachers being directly evaluated on the basis of pupil assessment came as a considerable shock and there were fears that the worst excesses of American accountability-through-testing-programmes would appear in this country. The National Union of Teachers was a powerful bloc on the APU's consultative committee and they insisted on the results of pupils and schools being kept strictly anonymous. In addition to this the APU followed the American national assessment model in using light sampling and matrix sampling. *Light sampling* meant that only small numbers of children in any chosen school were tested. *Matrix sampling* meant that, out of the total range of test items, each child was given only a manageable number and that children in the same school sat essentially different tests since they had different selections of items. These decisions, to use light sampling, matrix sampling and anonymity of pupils and schools, meant that in the end APU results could not be used to evaluate individual schools.

With the problems explained in Chapter 3 of measuring changes in performance over time, the APU's aim of monitoring standards, and thus the performance of schools in general, also became weakened. The test development teams, who were subject specialists rather than test development experts, concentrated instead on using the data for research purposes. Each of the three original survey areas, maths, language and science, completed an initial round of five annual surveys in 1982, 1983 and 1984 respectively. After this initial phase, the teams were commissioned to survey only every five years and to spend time in between surveys on dissemination and on making a more detailed analysis of their findings, for example, in relation to school and child background factors. This was referred to as 'mining the data'. For example, the maths team has done a lot of work on children's errors in maths, the science team similarly on children's understanding and misconceptions in science. Both teams have extended our knowledge of gender differences, while the language team has pioneered work on the assessment of oracy. The modern language surveys were used to develop training materials for teachers; and so on. There can be little doubt that the work of the APU's test development teams has produced a tremendous amount of information that is of use to teachers. It is ironic of course that this national assessment, which was greeted with such fear and concern by many in the teaching profession, became a research exercise with direct and valuable feedback to practitioners.

But, how then have schools been accounting for themselves over the last fifteen years, if APU national assessment has not been able to deliver the monitoring of school performance?

School self-evaluation

School self-evaluation (SSE) has been a major development. This trend began in the mid-1970s and the emphasis was on critical examination by schools of their own organisation, processes, and/or outcomes. It developed as a response to accountability demands, certainly, but was also concerned with teachers' professional development and with improving managerial efficiency. The process of self-evaluation also took a variety of forms: organisational analysis, process-oriented or issue-based approaches and checklists for self-review; the ILEA's 'Keeping the School Under Review' is perhaps the best known example of the latter. Despite these various purposes and approaches, in general the focus was, and is, on the institution: teacher development and pupil performance issues are considered in the context of whole-school policies (Simons, 1988).

This movement, with its emphasis on a professional body carrying out evaluation in its own terms to improve professional practice and understanding, was in reaction against managerial and productivity models of accountability, based on economic and administrative concerns for efficiency, tidiness and value for money (MacIntyre, 1989). Self-evaluation was perceived as an appropriate, professional, way for educationalists to respond to demands for public accountability.

A major issue for SSE in an accountability setting is, however, that although the outcomes of SSE *may* be made public, they are rarely read by the public. Indeed, in some LEAs there is concern that not even LEA staff read the (lengthy) SSE reports. For schools, however, the importance lies in the process, not the product. SSE is, therefore, largely an 'invisible' method of evaluating schools and is not generally in the public domain. Thus, by the early 1980s it became clear that professional, school-based self-evaluation was not acceptable to politicians (and many parents) as a basis for school evaluation in the era of 'value for money' and market place competition.

Publication of exam results

The next development came in the 1980 Education Act, when secondary schools were required to publish exam results. This Act was the first of the new Conservative Government's moves in education and a major plank of the Act was that parents using the state sector should have more information and choice in deciding which schools their children should attend. Thus, from 1982 the annual publication of public examination results (at 16 and 18) was made compulsory.

Reaction to this requirement to publish examination results was mixed: several of the teachers' unions objected on professional grounds, believing that the published information was likely to be misleading and to have a deleterious effect on the education provided by secondary schools; local authority organisations argued that the expense of providing the information could not be justified. On the other hand, there was a widespread belief that schools should be more accountable to the communities they serve and that the publication of examination results would help to bring this about.

There is no compulsion for schools to provide summary measures of these results, such as total number of passes and pass rates, although some may choose to do so. These regulations, governing the presentation of results, are designed to make school 'league tables' difficult to construct but certainly in London a national evening newspaper has published league tables of London's secondary schools based on exam results.

The problem with using examination results to evaluate school performance is that the nature of the intake to a school will have a critical effect on the examination results or 'output' measures. Schools do make a difference, but social background factors of the children such as poverty and parents' own level of education, have a strong effect.

There is a large body of literature showing that children from socially disadvantaged areas tend to have lower exam scores and test results than those from more socially advantaged areas (eg Coleman et al, 1966; DES, 1967; Rutter et al, 1979). Simple school test and exam averages will in part reflect these differences and the students' performance on intake, and thus obscure any real 'effects' due to the school.

As Goldstein and Cuttance (1988) point out, the attainment of the children entering a school is the single most important determinant of later achievement. So that if we are using assessment results to evaluate *school* performance by comparing one school with another, we must either make allowances for these background effects or look at progress scores (i.e. how much more the children can do at 16 than at 11) rather than actual exam results. Because secondary schools with intakes of mainly below-average pupils at eleven will not usually get, and indeed, cannot be expected to get, examination results which are as good as schools which get a large proportion of above-average pupils at eleven, researchers and LEAs began developing ways of analysing school examination results taking into account 'background variables' (see Plewis et al, 1981).

Considerable progress had been made by, among others, the

ILEA in this sort of analysis and indeed the ILEA's tables of school-average exam results were adjusted for intake measures for each school (Nuttall, 1988).

However, there are problems in using average school results to compare schools even if they are adjusted. The rank order of schools achieved after adjustment can vary considerably and apparently haphazardly by making trivial modifications to the adjustment procedures. Goldstein and Woodhouse (1988) found this for LEAs; the same effect has been found in ranking school districts (rather than schools) in Kentucky: changing or modifying criteria for ranking and for adjusting scores resulted in quite different rankings of school districts (Guskey and Kifer, 1989). It is also the case that rank order can change quite considerably from one year to the next. Furthermore, the limitation with ranking as a process is that, regardless of overall levels of performance, a ranking procedure always produces a top and a bottom, with little indication of what these mean in terms of performance. As the Kentucky study puts it: 'The ten shortest players in the National Basketball Association, for instance, are on average pretty tall.' The other problem is with using *average* measures since these averages tell us little. For example, two schools may get the same average results but have achieved them in different ways: one school may have good results for pupils whose attainments on intake were poor, but relatively low results for pupils whose attainment was high on intake, while the other may have more homogenous results for all its pupils. The *average* scores therefore are masking important information about the schools (Goldstein and Cuttance, *op cit*). If assessment results are to be used in order to make decisions about schools, then good quality information is needed and this means more than a rank order or league table based on averages.

Work carried out by the ILEA Research and Statistics Branch and the University of London Institute of Education (ULIE) has involved a much more detailed analysis which uses the results of *individual* pupils within schools. Using a new statistical method, each child's performance can be analysed in relation to his or her gender, ethnic group, attainment on entry to school, etc, rather than, as before, *school* average performance being analysed against school measures of its population. Multi-level data analysis techniques (Goldstein, 1987) allow the information about individual pupil attainment and characteristics to be analysed together with school level data, thus giving a much more sophisticated picture of how well schools are doing in relation to their intake. For example, the ILEA analysis was able to identify which schools are producing good results for certain groups of pupils. Some schools are much more effective than others at improving the performance of lower ability pupils, and of some groups of ethnic minority students (Nuttall *et al*, 1989). So these more complex analyses can help us to make a much more sophisticated evaluation of school effectiveness in academic areas.

However, the publication of secondary school exam results has not had as much of an effect on schools as perhaps might have been anticipated. Parents have had another piece of information on which to base their choice of school, but schools have not become obviously more 'efficient', nor has there been widespread closing down of schools with exam results that are perceived to be poor.

Performance indicators

As we have already seen, exam results or assessment levels only tell us about one aspect of schools; they constitute only a partial evaluation. The development of *performance indicators* is an attempt to remedy this. The idea is that the schools' performance and 'value for money' are calculated on the basis of a very wide range of factors including: pupil–teacher ratios, qualifications of staff, class management and teaching skills, teachers' commitment and professional attitudes, the quality of curricular management, management of time, students' engagement in the learning process, the quality of the learning experience, outcomes of learning, homework policy, attendance and punctuality, attitudes and behaviour including incidents of vandalism and graffiti, and costs per pupil (SIS, 1988). Of course, at a crude level, school performance indicators are nothing new. Exam results, sports results, even the annual school concert, have always been used by the public to evaluate schools. But the increasing emphasis on 'value for money', accountability, and parental choice has resulted in the development of more wide-ranging approaches to the evaluation of schools' performance.

However, developing sophisticated measures such as those listed above is clearly not going to be easy. A number of them require qualitative judgements to be made, for example, the quality of the learning experience, so they involve value judgements or subjective assessments rather than quantitative or numerical measures such as, for example, percentage of attendances. There does seem to be a commitment to including qualitative information, but some indicators do not lend themselves particularly well to measurement, and we know that where we have numerical and descriptive information, the quantitative data tends to overwhelm the qualitative information (House, 1978 *op cit*). It is easier to use numbers as a form of shorthand than to précis descriptions and use those. There are other complications too, for example, if a school does well on three indicators and poorly on another three indicators, what is it possible to say about the school overall?

Performance indicators are still in the development stage, but there is no doubt that the 'economics' model of evaluating schools is with us for the foreseeable future. Whether complex performance indicators are used, or whether simple league tables of schools on the basis of published national assessment results prevail, is hard to predict at this moment.

National curriculum assessment

Part of the function of the 1988 Education Reform Act was to strengthen parental choice, to widen the net of publication of assessment results to include primary schools, and to strengthen the market-place model with regard to the fate of 'popular' and 'unpopular' schools. The projected programme of national assessment to monitor the national curriculum is a very different exercise from the APU's national assessment. All children of 7, 11, 14 (and 16 for subjects not assessed via GCSE) will be assessed using tests and activities directly related to the national curriculum. Attainment targets, which are descriptions of knowledge and activities to be learned (that is what children should 'know, understand and be able to do'), are divided up into ten levels of performance covering the age range 7 to 16, and these are described by statements of attainment. Children will be assessed on these statements of attainment by a mixture of testing and teacher assessment, and this will give profiles of attainment, across the ten levels of performance, for individual children.

These profiles of attainment are to serve a formative assessment function at 7, 11 and 14—i.e. to guide the child's future teaching and learning programme. They will also be used as a basis for communication with parents; this detailed, structured information will no doubt be very valuable. This same detailed information will also, however, be summarised for publication and children will be assigned to one of the ten levels of attainment in each subject. Schools will have to publish distributions of performance on these levels at 11, 14 and 16, and may choose to at 7 as well.

Not only must results be made available for each school, but for the relevant classes they must be made available to parents and those responsible for the school. Results for the class may well emerge in the local area as measures of teacher effectiveness.

Whether the results will eventually form part of formal teacher appraisal is not yet clear. What is clear is that the published results will be used to evaluate schools. Although the DES states that 'LEAs will *not* be *required* to publish league tables' (DES, 1989a, their emphasis), neither will they be forbidden to do so. It seems highly likely that on the basis of the test scores, local league tables will in fact be constructed.

These school level results are *not* to be adjusted for socio-economic background of the intake. The main report of the Task Group on Assessment and Testing (TGAT) argued that using statistically adjusted results to compare schools' performance 'would be liable to lead to complacency if results were adjusted and to misinterpretation if they were not' (DES, 1988a). Instead, for each school, TGAT recommended that the results be set in the context of a written account of the work of the school as a whole, and socio-economic and other influences that are known to affect attainment.

There is a considerable amount of research on adjusting exam scores for intake and on measuring school effectiveness which TGAT simply ignored (Nuttall, 1988). The solution of TGAT, to publish results aggregated for the school in the context of a general report for the area . . . 'to indicate the nature of socio-economic and other influences which are known to affect schools', suggests that allowances may be made by parents and others, but at a much less precise level than that of statistical adjustment. Indeed, the responsibility for the interpretation is passed on to the audience, that is to parents and the general public.

The reason that statistical adjustment is not to be used is that if the comparison is a direct one parents can look for schools with *actual* high scores—which is what, the Government says, most parents want. This is of course partly true, but what this argument ignores is that sophisticated analysis of the type described earlier can tell us which schools are performing well for particular groups of pupils, e.g. girls/boys, ethnic minorities, etc, in which parents will most certainly be interested. Publication of adjusted *and* unadjusted scores would seem to be part of the solution.

As the assessments work their way through the system there will be data on 11-year-olds against which to analyse results at 14, data on 7-year-olds against which to analyse the scores of 11-year-olds and similarly for 14 and 16-year-olds; but for many schools damage to their image and popularity will have been done by then. There is of course scope for an individual LEA to choose to adjust its test results for intake, and many may well choose to do this in order to extract information which could help in understanding why some schools perform better than others.

The *aggregated* assessment results are to be made available in a standard format, so that each school's results can be set against those for the LEA as a whole. Eventually, LEAs themselves will be compared and evaluated: 'In due course, LEAs should also be required to submit to the Secretary of State data on distributions of attainment at the four key ages with comparisons over time for all schools they maintain, as the basis for compiling national data and so that the SEAC and the NCC can monitor standards of attainment . . .' (DES, 1988b, para 35).

But, to return to the subject of this chapter, will national curriculum assessment help to evaluate schools?

There is no doubt that the results will be an important factor in school evaluation, despite the danger that, unadjusted, they will be misleading and could result in the unjustified victimisation of schools in socially disadvantaged communities, while failing to locate the poorly performing schools in the socially advantaged communities. But as parents and teachers know, and the TGAT Report itself acknowledged, a school's performance can only be judged fairly by taking account of many aspects of its work, not just the academic. At the same time, however, the TGAT Report proposed setting up a highly significant assessment system with a requirement to publish. There is a real danger in such a system that *one indicator of performance* becomes *the* indicator, and then the goal itself.

We must be careful, however, to keep the evaluation of schools on the basis of test and exam results in perspective. If the main users of evaluation information in this setting are parents, there are two points that must be made. The first is that not all parents are able or willing to choose a school that is not the nearest one, so only some parents will make use of the assessment-based evaluation or performance indicators. Second, many parents are not looking for assessment results as the main or only criterion for choice of school. Particularly at primary level, parents are likely to be looking for a friendly, happy atmosphere, approachable staff, a supportive caring environment and an all-round approach to education, as well as evidence that the academic standards are good. So although we may be offended by unfair league tables, evaluating schools on the basis of national curriculum assessment results may have less of an effect on parental choice than is anticipated.

5

Equal Opportunities and Bias in Assessment

Let us begin this chapter by reiterating the fact that one of the reasons formal examining was first introduced in England was to promote equal opportunities: the Civil Service exams were introduced in the 1850s to permit advancement through talent rather than patronage. Just over 100 years later, in the USA, however, this view was challenged. Tests and exams were felt to be *denying* opportunities for advancement, particularly for black students. In the post-1965 Civil Rights legislation era, critics of 'advancement through testing' were pointing out that opportunities to acquire talent, or to be able to show it to sufficient effect in tests and exams, were not equally distributed (Wood, 1987). In other words, tests and exams could be biased.

It is also important to point out that both viewpoints continue to be held simultaneously, sometimes by the same individual. Thus, one might argue that the eleven-plus and public exams are important as a means of equalising opportunities and as a necessary corrective to patronage, while at the same time understanding that tests and exams may be biased in favour of one particular gender, social or ethnic group.

The argument in relation to IQ testing has been examined by Mackintosh and Mascie-Taylor for the Swann Report:

> 'Perhaps the most contentious assumption underlying the whole argument, however, is that IQ tests could ever provide a fair measure of the intelligence of children from working-class families, let alone those from ethnic or racial minorities. Devised by white middle-class psychologists, standardised on white children, validated by their

ability to predict performance in white schools, IQ tests, it is argued, will inevitably reflect white, middle-class values, must be biased against other groups, and could not possibly provide a realistic assessment of their abilities. The argument may seem reasonable and persuasive. But it needs examination to disentangle what is possibly true from what is probably misleading: ... If a child has been deprived of intellectual stimulation or educational opportunity, it is small wonder that his intellectual performance will reflect this fact. An IQ test is no more able to gauge a child's true innate potential regardless of the circumstances of his upbringing than is a pair of scales to measure his true potential weight regardless of what he has been fed. To repeat: IQ tests measure a sample of a child's actual behaviour, what he knows and has learned. Some children may have lacked the opportunity to acquire the knowledge crucial for answering certain questions, just as a starved child may have been fed a diet lacking critical nutrients. To claim that IQ tests are biased is often only a way of making the point that IQ tests measure skills and knowledge which not all children may have been able to acquire; in other words, that differences in IQ scores are partly due to differences in the environmental experiences of different children.'

(Mackintosh and Mascie-Taylor, 1985 Annex D, Swann Report)

This quotation makes clear that there are two different issues at stake. Wood refers to these as the opportunity to acquire talent and the opportunity to show it to good effect (Wood, 1987 *op cit*). It is important to see the issues of unequal access to learning (the opportunity to acquire talent) and bias in assessment (the opportunity to show it to good effect) as separate.

In the 1970s and 1980s in Britain most of the discussion has focused on gender, social class and to a lesser extent ethnic differences in performance, for example, girls' performance in the eleven-plus in Birmingham and Northern Ireland (*TES*, 8 July, 88 and *Independent*, 16 October, 87) and social class differences in public exam performance. There has been some discussion of bias in assessment in relation to gender (APU, 1988; Murphy, 1989), but little discussion of bias in relation to ethnic group.

However, over the next five to ten years, with the advent of national assessment, which will be so crucial in determining children's life chances, it is vital that we pay far more attention to *all* the bias issues in assessment.

First we will look at the evidence about gender and ethnic differences in performance, then at some of the reasons for these differences; finally we will look at the technical issues involved in avoiding bias in test design.

Differences in performance

Gender

This issue has been reviewed by Harvey Goldstein for the Equal Opportunities Commission (EOC). I will summarise the evidence here and refer the interested reader to the full report (Goldstein, 1988).

Language

The early longitudinal research which studied groups of children through a period of schooling (Douglas *et al*, 1968; Davie *et al*, 1972; Fogelman *et al*, 1978) showed boys to be superior in vocabulary knowledge at eleven, and reading comprehension advantages to be in favour of girls at 7, reducing by age 11 and reversing to show a small advantage to boys by 16. However, more recent APU data gives girls superior overall performance in reading at 11 and 15. A complication in interpreting this apparently contradictory data is that the APU assessments are of a quite different type from the standardised tests used in the longitudinal studies. In writing, too, girls do better than boys at 11 and 15 on APU tests.

Mathematics

Early studies using standardised maths tests involving mostly arithmetical items show boys and girls performing similarly at 11 and with boys outperforming girls at 15 (Douglas, *op cit*). However, APU tests which include a much wider range of items show girls performing better than boys on solely computational tasks, with boys better at measurement and practical tasks, and very little difference between them in problem-solving tasks. At 15 there are only very small differences in number skills and algebra, but girls do less well at measurement and spatial topics, applied and practical maths (APU, 1986).

Science

It is in science that attainment differences are most marked. APU data – which is the most comprehensive science data we have and covers primary as well as secondary levels – show that all differences are in favour of boys: at 11 in the application of taught science concepts, at 13 applying physics concepts, at 15 applying physics concepts together with use of equipment, interpreting data and reading information. The APU tested a sample of children regardless of their exposure to science and of course part of these differences, particularly at 15, are because boys have had more exposure to these topics than girls. This is quite aside from any 'boy-friendly' features of the science assessments.

Verbal and non-verbal reasoning

There is fairly limited and dated evidence on these beyond the age of 11. What evidence there is from the longitudinal studies mentioned earlier is that by the end of secondary school boys score somewhat higher on the non-verbal tests than girls. At 11, it is generally recognised that girls score considerably higher on the verbal tests and higher on the non-verbal tests than boys, and girls continue to do better on verbal tests at secondary level.

Public exams

The English School Leavers Survey 1983/4 shows that in 1984, for the first time, more girls than boys got an A-level pass, while at 16, 11 per cent of girls left school with five or more O-levels compared with 9.1 per cent of boys (DES, 1986). The figures for 1986/7 show that overall 58 per cent of girls compared with 51 per cent of boys got at least one O-level at grade A to C, or CSE grade 1. Ten years previously it was 53 per cent and 50 per cent respectively (DES, 1989b). Figures from the ILEA for the period 1985–1987 confirm girls' overall superior performance, but with variation across schools. Girls in ILEA secondary schools achieved on average the equivalent of one grade 3 CSE pass more than boys, but in some schools the difference was negligible, while in others it amounted to one extra pass at nearly an A grade. So, clearly, the school itself has some effect on girls' and boys' differential performance (*Guardian*, 4.7.89, p. 21).

What is almost more significant, however, is the *pattern* of passes. Proportionately more girls qualify in arts subjects and more boys in science subjects because girls tend to choose arts and boys sciences. In A-level the vast majority of passes in maths, physics, computer studies and economics go to boys. This, of course, limits girls' access to many higher status jobs and professions.

The 1986/7 School Leavers Survey (DES, 1989b *op cit*) shows that at O-level/CSE the gap in gender subject choice was closing (on the back of compulsory science to 16, and initiatives to get girls into science and technology) but girls are still way behind boys in higher grade passes in maths, physics and CDT at O-level/CSE, and maths and physics at A-level. By contrast, more girls than boys passed English, biology, French, creative arts and history. However the

1988 GCSE results show that girls have increased their share of A–C grades over boys compared with 1985 figures for O-level and CSE, in English, French, history, religious studies *and* physics, although not yet in maths (Nuttall, personal communication).

Ethnic group

Some of the earliest information about differences in performance by ethnic groups in Britain came from the work of Michael Rutter and colleagues (Rutter *et al*, 1974; Yule *et al*, 1975). They found that West Indian children had lower average reading scores than 'indigenous' children of the same age, and that the length of time the West Indian children had been in the UK made a difference to their performance.

The National Child Development Study reported in 1979 that, at 16, West Indian children scored lower than 'indigenous' groups in reading and maths (Essen and Ghodsian, 1979) and that, in general, ethnic minority children who were born in the UK performed considerably better than those who were born abroad.

The ILEA also carried out literacy surveys between 1968 and 1976, finding that pupils of West Indian origin and Cypriots had poorer reading test scores than other groups (Little, 1975; Mabey, 1981). More worryingly, the longitudinal analysis of this data showed that while the performance of what were by then called 'Black British' students was significantly lower at 8, by school leaving age it was relatively lower still.

An early study looking at the organisation of multi-racial schools found that relatively few students were entered for public exams and, when they were, it was for CSE rather than O-level (Townsend and Brittan, 1972). The Rampton Report found that, in six LEAs with high proportions of ethnic minority children, pupils from West Indian families achieved fewer high grades in O-level and CSE English and maths than either Asian or indigenous white children (Rampton, 1981). Asian children performed slightly better than both other groups in maths *and* in overall number of passes at both O-level/CSE and A-level.

The Swann Report which followed on from the Rampton Report found that again West Indian children performed less well than the other two groups at O-level/CSE, but that their performance had improved compared with the figures obtained for the earlier report (Swann, 1985).

A later study looking at the performance of pupils of white, South Asian and Afro-Caribbean origin in 23 comprehensive schools in six

LEAs (Eggleston *et al*, 1986) found that white students were still more likely to be entered for O-level than ethnic minority students. As for exam performance, the picture varied across and within LEAs, but overall the performance of white and South Asian pupils was similar, with Afro-Caribbean boys gaining significantly fewer high grade passes.

A study (Smith and Tomlinson, 1989) of performance in multi-racial comprehensives found that patterns of performance are very different in different schools. Overall, however, the Asian and West Indian children were behind at 11 and 13 but were catching up with white pupils by the time they sat O-level/CSE exams at 16. Specifically, Muslim children of Bangladeshi and Pakistani origin scored substantially below average on reading and maths at 11, while Sikhs and Hindus scored average or above. West Indian children scored below average but higher than the low-scoring South Asian group. After two years this gap widened; at this point allocation to exam classes was made and white children were allocated to more, higher level exams. Over the next three years the ethnic minority students caught up, although the West Indian performance in maths remained poor. However, these children's exam results in English were rather better than those of white British children.

By contrast, the ILEA analysis of public exam results for 1985 and 1986 showed that after taking into account differences in verbal reasoning ability and sex, the performance of students of Pakistani, Indian, Greek and South-East Asian origin was better than that of students of English, Scottish or Welsh (ESW) background (ILEA, 1987). As with the gender differences in the ILEA analysis and the ethnic group differences referred to in the above study, there was considerable variation from school to school. For example the average difference in performance between Pakistani and ESW students was equivalent to an O-level grade A pass, but this varied from almost no difference in some schools to the equivalent of about two B grades in others.

These studies are more sophisticated than the early ones, in that they use a more complex statistical analysis which takes account of more background factors and is able to analyse at the student and school level, rather than at just the school level using aggregated data. They also usually have a more sophisticated categorisation of ethnic group than just 'Asian' or 'West Indian', which of course ignores the enormous linguistic and cultural spread within these groups. What they seem to be showing is that the performance gap between ESW and ethnic minority students is much less significant, indeed in some cases is reversed, relative to the mid-1970s.

What they also show is that some of these differences in performance are due to effects of the school. We now turn to a consideration of these differences: how much is due to bias in assessment (equal opportunity to show talent) and how much is due to differential access and cultural factors (equal opportunity to acquire talent).

Reasons for differences in performance

The reasons for these differences are of course complex and by no means fully understood. But one obvious explanation for the differential success in public exams is different entry patterns: ethnic minority students were, as we have seen prior to GCSE, being allocated more to CSE than the higher status O-level. It will be interesting to know whether the same is happening with allocation to higher level, or more difficult, exams in the GCSE subjects which have differentiated exam papers. Girls, too, have been differentially allocated to CSE in maths: as Valerie Walkerdine's work showed (Walden and Walkerdine, 1985), girls and boys who did equally well on maths tests were differentially allocated to O-level or CSE because girls were seen by their teachers as 'not *really* bright' and 'working to their full potential' while the boys were seen as 'really bright' but 'underachieving'! The EOC also has evidence of girls being similarly differentially allocated by their teachers to the easier routes in GCSE maths (*Observer*, 2 October, 1988).

The case-study work of Cecile Wright, within Eggleston's study described above, showed that Afro-Caribbean students were likely to be placed in bands and examination sets well below their actual academic ability. Her evidence suggested that the teachers' assessment of these students was influenced more by behavioural criteria than cognitive ones (Wright, 1987). This was a result of the teachers' 'adverse relationship' with these students and the outcome was of course to limit their educational opportunities. Schools admitted on several occasions that this was an allocation based not only on ability, but also on 'social factors': they were not prepared to put black children into the academic/examination streams in case they were disruptive or unrealistically ambitious (Eggleston, 1988). Even in the most 'egalitarian' schools the researchers found that the teachers had low expectations of the Asian and Afro-Caribbean children. In the ILEA Junior School study too, there was a tendency for some Afro-Caribbean children to be allocated by their teachers to the middle verbal reasoning ability band when in fact their test scores showed them to be in the top band (Mortimore *et al*, 1988). There is a host of literature on the self-fulfilling nature of low teacher expectation. Indeed, in two case-study schools in Eggleston's research, Afro-Caribbean children entered at 11 with reading test results on a par with or higher than the Asian and white children; five years later only one Afro-Caribbean child in each school (out of 19 and 36) was entered for five or more O-levels, i.e. 5.3 per cent and 2.7 per cent respectively, compared with 24.5 per cent and 18.5 per cent for white children (Eggleston *et al*, 1986).

So it seems that the effect of stereotypes and low expectations for girls and ethnic minority students can be to limit their educational experience. Thus, they are denied the opportunity to acquire talent.

But what about factors in the assessments themselves, providing the opportunity to *show* talent? Most obviously, if the language of the assessment is not the first language or dialect of the children tested, they will be at a disadvantage (ILEA, 1983). If the assessment material is couched in the culture of one group, children from other groups will similarly be at a disadvantage. An example from a First World War intelligence test, the Army Beta test, gives a nice illustration: non-English speaking immigrants to the USA were asked to point out what was missing from a set of pictures, one of which showed a tennis court with the net missing. The immigrant who could not answer this question (and others) correctly was deemed to be of low intelligence whereas the truth might have been that he had never seen a tennis court.

This is not just a one-off bizarre example from pre-war America. In a recent study in Britain, researchers using a popular standardised reading test with bilingual, working class and middle class children of primary school age found that much of the material was culturally alien to the first two groups. Thus, what was being assessed was not only reading, but also their understanding of English middle class culture. For example, one item went like this:

Jimmy _____ tea, because he was our guest.

    1) washed the dishes after
    2) was late for
    3) got the best cake at
    4) could not eat his

(Hannon and McNally, 1986)

The researchers found that virtually all the middle class children answered this 'correctly', while 60 per cent of both the working class sample and the bilingual group did not: their most popular choice of answer was not (3) but (1). The authors argue that the convention of having children to tea and giving the guest the best cake is a middle class one, and so other groups of children are disadvantaged by this item. The test had a number of items, not just this one, which relied on particular cultural understandings and experiences; they conclude that the test is culturally biased. Clearly, on a test like this, bilingual and non-middle class English speaking children do not have the same opportunity to show their true ability to read.

What is interesting is how little recognition has been given, in the UK at least, to bias in the assessments as a factor in differential measured performances of various groups.

We know that boys do better than girls when the questions are of the multiple-choice type, and this is reversed with free-response or essay questions (Murphy, 1982; Wood, 1978). There is also evidence, from O-level English language exams (Wood, 1978) that, not surprisingly, boys do better than girls when the topic of the question is a 'masculine' one and girls better when it is a 'feminine' one. Of course, boys' apparent dislike of extended essay writing (especially that which involves self-reflection or empathy) may well be part of the process which puts them on the route towards choice of maths and sciences, while girls may be 'turned off' the more de-personalised modes of communication in these subjects (APU, 1988). 'Free' choice of subject is never quite 'free'.

In theory, what this means is that we could design assessments that favour (i.e. are biased in favour of) one particular group. By using all multiple-choice questions we could advantage boys, by using all free-response questions with 'feminine' topics we could advantage girls, by using material which relates to one specific cultural group we can advantage them. This issue is rarely discussed, presumably because it smacks of social engineering and raises a host of difficult questions.

Thanks to the work of the APU and Patricia Murphy we know more about the factors which affect girls' performance. But we are still a long way from being able to develop assessments that are fairly balanced as far as girl-friendly and boy-friendly items are concerned (and no mention of balancing for social class and cultural group). What Patricia Murphy's work has shown is, not only that girls' performance in traditionally male subjects like physics can be improved by changing, for example, the measuring apparatus so that they can see the relevance of the activity (*TES*, 13 Jan, 89, p. 4), but that girls and boys tend to perceive a problem in different ways. Boys tend to abstract the problem from the context, while girls attend to the totality of the problem context, focusing on more clues than do the boys, which may be one reason why girls do less well than boys in multiple choice tests (Murphy, 1989).

'Speaking freely to the teacher' which was an early version of a statement of attainment for English would have caused problems in national curriculum assessment for many children. For some ethnic groups there will be cultural inhibitions in this task—after all there are many *parents* who hesitate to speak freely to teachers. 'Social, cultural, class factors, and indeed the effects of racism, mean that speaking freely to teachers is not something that comes easily to a large part of the population' (Nuttall, 1989a).

Avoiding bias in test design

There are two ways in which test developers can address bias. They look for:

- *item content bias:* where there is bias perceived by users through examining the content.
- *statistical item bias:* where items or questions favour one or other group disproportionately (Smith and Whetton, 1988). This is also called differential item functioning.

 Both of these biases can be addressed during test development. The TGAT Report advocates looking for both sorts of bias, i.e. doing an item content 'sensitivity' review as well as a statistical analysis, when developing material for national assessment. In the USA this is now standard practice.

 Item content bias would be detected by males and females and members of different ethnic groups reviewing items for gender bias, racial stereotypes or any material which could be offensive to a particular group. Statistical item bias is examined to determine whether any questions are disproportionately difficult for a particular group once that group's overall test performance has been taken into account. For example, 'car is to tyre as (tank) is to caterpillar' was disproportionately easy for boys in one test, while 'dough is to pizza as (pastry) is to pie' was disproportionately easy for girls (Smith and Whetton, *op cit*).

 In America there is a 'Code of Fair Testing Practices in Education' which the major testing agencies apparently follow. This requires them to indicate for all tests and assessments 'the nature of the evidence obtained concerning the appropriateness of each test for groups of different racial, ethnic or linguistic backgrounds . . .' (JCTP, 1988), and demands that 'Test developers should strive to make tests that are as fair as possible for test takers of different races, gender, ethnic backgrounds, or handicapping conditions'. This has to be a step in the right direction. The code has nevertheless met with a certain amount of scepticism in America, largely because of the lack of any measures for enforcement. As a former Assistant Secretary of Education put it:

> 'If all the maxims are followed I have no doubt the overall quotient of goodness and virtue should be raised. Like Moses, the test-makers

have laid down ten commandments they hope everyone will obey.
That doesn't work very well in religion—adultery continues.' (*TES*,
25 November, 88)

However, there *has* been litigation over assessment in the USA,
the most relevant being the suit the Golden Rule Insurance Company brought against Educational Testing Services (the equivalent
of Britain's NFER) which develops insurance licensing exams. The
Golden Rule Company alleged that this test was discriminatory to
blacks. The case was settled out of court in 1984 by an agreement,
the key provision of which was that preference should be given in
test construction to items that showed smaller differences in black
and white performance. This has come to be called the Golden Rule
Strategy, and the Golden Rule Bias Reduction Principle (Weiss,
1987) states that 'among questions of equal difficulty and validity in
each content area, questions which display the least differences in
passing rates between majority and minority test takers should be
used first'.
However, by 1987 the ETS president recanted on the 1984
agreement and the issue is now hotly disputed. The contention
centres around the point that relying on group differences in
performance on test questions as indicators of 'bias' ignores the
possibility that such differences may validly reflect real differences
in knowledge or skill (Faggen, 1987).
So far we have been talking about making an analysis of bias in
relation to individual items. It is also possible, however, to look for
test bias, i.e. where the average scores for various groups differ on
the test as a whole. The difficulty here lies in separating true bias
from a valid reflection of reality. If a test shows average differences
between groups, it may be that these really exist. The question
could be phrased: if people of equal ability from different groups
take the test will they get the same result?
But, of course that begs the question of what we mean by true
'ability' in a subject; definitions tend to be culture dependent.
Goldstein (1986) points out, as we have already discussed, that we
could design new tests to advantage either gender (or indeed any
ethnic or socio-economic group) by manipulating the type and
nature of items used. For example, we know that girls do particularly well on verbal reasoning tests, so to develop an 'apparently'
unbiased verbal reasoning test we would have to load it with items
that were biased *against* the girls, e.g. including items using traditionally male vocabulary. Smith and Whetton argue that this would
reduce the validity of the test: by deliberately using words known
only to one group we would *increase bias*, even if the end result was
an equal mean score for all groups. Verbal reasoning tests must be

made to measure reasoning processes using word knowledge as the medium, and word knowledge that is common to all test takers, rather than known to only one group.

There are two general points to make here: not only is this a very complex and contentious area, but also how far behind the Americans we are in dealing with bias in assessment. It may not be possible to have completely culture-fair or unbiased assessments, but test developers and Exam Boards have to be as certain as they can that tests measure relevant knowledge differences between test takers and not irrelevant, culturally specific factors. *Group* score differences do reflect a host of causes, including genuine knowledge differences and test-taking abilities, but they should not be due to the use of irrelevant and biased questions. As the Director of the Fair Test Organisation in the USA, quoted in Chapter 1, points out, standardised multiple-choice exams have become America's cradle-to-grave arbiter of social mobility, so control over the fairness and validity of these exams is crucial (Weiss, 1987).

The main TGAT Report (DES, 1988a) says disappointingly little on equal opportunities and bias. There are 21 lines which recommend that, where necessary and practical, assessments be carried out in the pupil's first language and that assessment items be reviewed for bias in respect of gender and race. This review, it says, should be carried out both by panels of teachers and by using statistical techniques. The group received the report on testing and equal opportunities from the EOC which was referred to at the start of this chapter, but this report was appended and its message largely ignored in the body of TGAT.

It is now commonly accepted good practice for test constructors to ensure that their instruments contain no sexual or racial stereotypes and we can assume that the national assessment development teams will pay attention to this. It is not so clear, however, how easy it will be for them to make the statistical analysis for item bias, and interpret any results sensibly, given the complex nature of SATs. As with much in national assessment we will have to wait and see. Clearly the balance of the form of question (essay type, structured question, practical task) will be crucial to equal opportunities, as will the context and content of the tasks (girl-friendly *vs* boy-friendly).

Given what we have said about teacher stereotypes of certain groups of children, it does seem crucial that this is addressed in in-service and pre-service training, particularly with regard to the continuous teacher assessment element of national assessment. On the plus side, since these assessments will be tied to specific tasks and statements of attainment, there is likely to be less room for stereotyping than in the more global judgements which in the past formed the bulk of teacher assessment and ratings of children.

We will return to a consideration of these issues in relation to national curriculum assessment in the final chapter.

6

Assessment at Primary Level

The assessment issues at primary level are quite different from those at secondary level. The emphasis has been on standardised tests rather than exams, and the testing of basic skills, particularly reading, predominates.

Introduction

Since the reduction in the eleven-plus, assessment at primary level has been very much for professional purposes: for feedback on teaching, identifying children with special needs or delays in learning, and for record-keeping; while assessment at secondary level has continued to be dominated by the selection and certification functions of public exams at 16 and 18.

There are two levels of assessment in primary schools: tests which the LEA requires its schools to do, and assessments which the school chooses to carry out. Our surveys in 1980 and 1983 (which are described in Chapter 3) showed that many LEAs require their schools to test children, mostly at 7, 9 and 11. The 1980 survey, which asked LEAs about standardised testing programmes *in general*, found that at least 79 per cent of all LEAs were doing some such testing. Reading was the most commonly tested skill, with maths and verbal reasoning in second place. Testing at 7 and 8 was common, but 11 was the most popular age for this testing (Gipps *et al*, 1983). The 1983 survey, by contrast, asked about testing programmes for *screening* purposes, and found that at least 71 per cent of all LEAs required schools to test at primary level for this purpose. Again reading was the most commonly tested skill, although infant checklists were also used quite widely. Testing at 7 and 8 was most common for screening purposes, with 11 the next most popular age (Gipps *et al*, 1987). (The differences between the 1980 and 1983 surveys are to be expected, since screening is traditionally carried out at a younger age and is more likely to include reading than verbal reasoning tests). A number of LEAs also assessed children at six (22 LEAs) and five (18 LEAs).

One point which emerges is that assessing children at 7, and indeed younger than this, is not the new phenomenon that the anxiety over national assessment at 7 might suggest. Of course there are a number of ways in which the current assessment and the national assessments differ, and it may be these that are causing anxiety, but we should not forget that there is a considerable amount of testing going on already. We will look at some national assessment issues later in this chapter.

We also found that, on top of this LEA-imposed testing, many primary schools choose to use other tests: 86 per cent of the 80 primary schools visited in the second stage of our 1980 survey, used tests with whole age groups of children on top of those required by the LEA. This picture of widespread testing at primary level is supported by information from other sources: HMI statistics suggest that over 90 per cent of primary schools test reading in some way and over 70 per cent test maths in some form. NFER-Nelson, one of the largest test publishers, sold enough test material in 1987 to test about three million children! (*TES*, 4 March, 88, p. 51). The most popular tests were again reading, maths and general ability, for each of which they estimate about 800,000 primary age children could have been tested.

At school level there are different assessment approaches, and it is quite likely that there is a variety of practice *within* individual schools: Murphy (1987) suggests that it . . . 'seems(s) to be fairly typical for primary schools not to have an explicitly stated whole-school assessment policy'. The policy is rather to let individual teachers adopt their own approach; where informal assessments are made, the recording of these may well be brief. A study of record-keeping in primary schools by Clift and others (1981) found that quite often records provided only very partial information about the child's achievements.

We know too that many teachers regard records as rather a chore to complete and make little use of those passed on by other teachers. This is related to a view commonly held by teachers, that 'any good teacher' can quickly form his or her own assessment of children when they start to teach them, and in any case they prefer to give children a fresh start rather than to allow past experiences to colour their view (Murphy, 1987; Gipps *et al*, 1983).

There are two problems with this attitude, however. The first is that it is a waste of everyone's time to ignore previous records of children: a more positive view of teacher assessment might be that teachers could maximise the benefits of their colleagues' insights by reading the records of children who come up to them.

The second is that without proper records the information which is passed from one teacher to the next is likely to be of a general nature, about the child's overall ability, rather than specific information related to what the child can and cannot do.

The problem with general 'overall assessments' of children is that we have conflicting evidence about how good teachers are at making these. In the ILEA Junior School Study, Mortimore and colleagues (Mortimore *et al*, 1988) found that the judgements of junior teachers were 'accurate' in that they were generally consistent with test scores (although this begs the question as to how accurate were the test scores). By contrast, a number of other studies draw attention to the fact that primary school teachers are *not* particularly accurate in estimating what children know, their future potential, or even how they rank with respect to each other (e.g. Tizard *et al*, 1988; Bennett *et al*, 1984; Hart *et al*, 1989). This is an important issue, for a number of reasons. First, a teacher's judgement of a pupils' progress affects the curriculum that is offered. Second, the gender, social class and appearance of the child can have a stereotyping effect on teachers' judgement. And third, there is the self-fulfilling prophecy that enhanced teacher expectation improves pupil performance and, more importantly, that low teacher expectation limits pupil performance, as the previous chapter showed only too clearly.

However, these findings generally relate to situations in which teachers are asked for informal and unspecific ratings. When teachers are asked to make more specific judgements of children's ability and understanding in relation to a list of *criteria*, it is likely that they will be less affected by stereotype and surface effects such as neatness of work, pleasantness of manner, etc. As Norman Thomas, ex-Chief Inspector for primary schools, put it: 'Observation is rarely good in any field unless the observer has a clear idea of what might be noticed and how that fits into the general context' (Thomas, 1982). The type of assessment required of teachers in national assessment is of course of this more specific sort: teacher assessment is made in relation to the detailed statements of attainment. Now we shall turn to some specific issues.

Screening

The term *screening* is borrowed from medicine: populations are screened in order to identify early a population at risk, which can then be given preventative treatment. For example, there is screening of all new-born babies for PKU (phenyl-ketonurea), a condition of the digestive system, which if untreated can lead to mental retardation. If identified early, however, and if a special diet is given to the child, retardation can be avoided.

This same principle – early identification followed by intervention, which prevents a harmful condition from developing – was adopted by health and social services in developing 'at risk' registers, and by education in developing screening and early identification procedures. Despite some contention about the predictive accuracy of screening in education, it has come to be a regular feature of LEA policy at primary level. LEAs do not see screening necessarily as a predictive exercise however, but rather as a detection strategy.

The assessment procedures used often involve checklists and rating scales. These rely on teacher assessment of individual children's progress, rather than the children themselves doing a test. The skills assessed are in various developmental areas including reading and pre-reading, number, language and social development. Part of the aim behind these checklists and scales is to make teachers aware of, and focus on, what children can and cannot do. The assessment is curriculum-related, so that teachers have immediate feedback on what to teach next or which areas need covering again; they are essentially for sensitising teachers to children's development. These procedures are criterion-referenced in that they contain lists of what children can and cannot do. There is often some arbitrary level set, and a performance below this indicates that further follow up or provision for special needs may be required.

More commonly than checklists, though, standardised reading tests are used in LEA screening programmes. This is not surprising considering the central role of reading in primary schools and the nature of most of the special help offered to the children identified. Interestingly, the test score or checklist result is rarely used *alone* to make a final identification of children for special help: the teacher's views and judgement about the child's needs are nearly always taken in to account. In our 1983 study, when we asked *teachers* how they identified children as needing help from outside, the child's progress (or lack of it) was the main indicator mentioned by almost half the teachers, while test scores were mentioned by only five per cent (12) of them, though of course test scores might have contributed to the teachers' views of the children's progress.

Screening, then is a widespread and fairly uncontentious activity.

The assessment of reading

It should be clear by now that reading is the most widely assessed subject, or skill, at primary level. However, there is considerable controversy over the best way to assess reading. Traditionally, the formal assessment of reading has been by standardised test. In a survey carried out in 1973 for the Bullock Report, the Schonell *Graded Word Reading Test* (GWRT) and Young's *Group Reading Test* were the most popular tests used; by 1980 our survey found that Young's was by far the most popular test in use. There were, however, a total of 36 different reading tests listed over the two surveys (Gipps and Wood, 1981).

There has been a clear shift in the type of test used from the early 1970s to the late 1980s. Early examples involved the single word read aloud (as in the Schonell GWRT); more recent tests involve reading for comprehension 'real' material and carrying out a *range* of reading tasks (as in the *Edinburgh Reading Tests*, for example). These changes, in what is held to be appropriate test content and mode, can be related to changes in popularly held models of reading.

When reading tests first started to appear in the 1940s, models of reading were based on decoding, and teaching emphasised performance rather than comprehension, so the first reading tests involved the reading aloud of single words. It has taken a long time for this sort of test to fade away: in 1975 the Bullock Report advocated using tests that assessed meaning rather than an artificial reading aloud for 'pronunciation'. By 1980 we found six LEAs still requiring the Schonell GWRT to be used and a great many individual schools still using it. By 1983, however, only two LEAs were using the Schonell in their screening programmes.

Since the era of the graded word reading test (so-called because the words to be read were arranged in order of increasing difficulty), models of reading have tended to move towards those which emphasise the process of reading as a whole rather than one aspect (e.g. decoding) and are more concerned with comprehension. Reading tests followed this route and moved towards involving sentences and then passages to test comprehension. Sentence reading tests, usually involve selecting the word required to complete a sentence from a list of alternatives. The criticism of tests like these is that they employ a type of discourse, that is a series of unrelated sentences, which bears no relation to the kind of writing encountered in real reading. Tests in which the child has to read passages usually contain questions about the passage content; criticism of the passage-and-comprehension-question type of test hinges on the fact that often the questions are more difficult to read than the passage, and that one can sometimes answer the questions without recourse to the text.

Some of the most recent reading tests assess comprehension of passages using the 'cloze' or 'fill-the-gap' technique: this involves giving the child a text with some words removed, which she or he then has to deduce from the context. The popularity of this technique among researchers and theorists is due to a belief that this test task is closest to the 'real' process of reading, which depends heavily on use of context clues. The cloze technique is, however, less popular among teachers because they are unhappy with the amount of 'guessing' involved.

There are a number of arguments against using tests of *any* kind to assess children's reading. These include:

- many tests are out of date
- most reading tests provide little or no diagnostic information
- tests cannot measure 'real reading' (Stierer, 1989)
- how do we interpret, or make sense of, the score? (see the quote from Andrew Stibbs in Chapter 2).
- many tests are linguistically and culturally biased (see the account of Hannon and McNally's work in Chapter 5) (Laycock, 1989)
- one cannot test the reading process as a unitary whole because this would have to include the social relationship between teacher and pupil
- emphasising testing de-skills the teacher by taking decisions about reading ability outside the teachers' judgement.

The first three points are to a certain extent answerable since the production of a number of new tests which *do* attempt to cover a range of real reading activities and some of which do provide diagnostic information. A good review of reading tests can be found in Vincent (1985).

As a result of these criticisms and of the development of more dynamic models of reading, there has been a move towards more informal methods of assessing reading (Raban, 1983). Informal reading inventories have been developed which help teachers to assess which skills pupils have mastered. These inventories can include checklists to assess attitudes to reading, checklists of examples to assess phonic skills (e.g. knowledge of initital and final letters), lists of books read by the pupil, activities to assess comprehension, and 'miscue' techniques for analysing reading aloud.

Miscue analysis is essentially a formalised structure for hearing children read, a device which primary schools traditionally use in the teaching of reading. Using miscue analysis, reading aloud develops from being a practising activity to a more diagnostic one. The teacher has a list of the most common errors children make, with a set of probable causes. By noticing and recording in a systemic way the child's errors and analysing the possible causes, teachers can correct misunderstandings, help the child develop appropriate strategies and reinforce skills. In other words miscue analysis is essentially an informal diagnostic assessment.

In the late 1980s the ILEA has produced a *Primary Language Record*. This is a detailed recording and observation document which is filled in at several points during the school year, so that the information can inform teaching, i.e. it is designed as a formative assessment rather than an administrative record. The assessment includes, indeed begins with, the parents' comments about the child's speech, writing and reading activities. There is also a section for recording the child's view of him/herself as a reader, writer and language user: the 'conference' between teacher and child here encourages the child to begin the process of self-assessment, something which is a key feature of profiles and records of achievement. The reading assessment is about as different from a standardised reading test as it is possible to be: it is based on teacher assessment and it requires predominently a written account of the child's interest in reading, enjoyment, strategies, difficulties, etc. There are also two rating scales for assessing performance in a more structured way. Both scales are scored from one to five, one assesses fluency and the other the child's range of reading experience. The Record, being open-ended, allows for the recording of language experiences in languages other than English where this is not the child's mother tongue. As an optional part of the scheme the teacher is given an observational guide to provide a framework for recording progress.

I have described the ILEA *Primary Language Record* in some detail because it is a good example of some of the newer approaches to assessment. It is child-focused rather than norm- or statistics-focused; it involves the child in making an assessment; it involves discussion between teacher and child; it allows for detailed recording and collection of samples or work; it is essentially a formative assessment.

The eleven-plus and after

The era of the eleven-plus was the heyday of the standardised test in primary schools. Not only did the exam itself contain a battery of tests, but children were prepared for it by taking tests regularly.

The proportion of children going on to grammar schools was the criterion by which many parents and many teachers judged the 'success' of a primary school. Inside the primary school the existence of the examination encouraged streaming and militated against mixed ability teaching. It inhibited work on topics which engaged more than one skill and encouraged concentration on examination-type work, including practice in intelligence tests.

It is not just in Britain that the demands of assessment can affect schooling. In France a 'dull, repetitive and harsh pedagogy' prevails in primary schools, with teachers sticking very closely to the curriculum laid down for fear of pupils failing their end-of-year assessments and being held back (Broadfoot and Osborn, 1987). This dreaded *'redoublement'* was formally abolished in France in the mid-sixties but continues to operate. In Germany, where an all-pervading grading system operates each year, British HMI found little evidence of individuality or originality in the children's work, although the German primary teachers said that they encouraged and accepted it (HMI, 1986). It seems that the grading is too important to allow much scope for straying from the curriculum.

The ending of the eleven-plus, which began in 1965 with the introduction of comprehensive secondary schooling, had a very significant effect on primary education in Britain. Freed from the constraints of a restrictive leaving exam the curriculum opened out, different methods of grouping developed and styles of pedagogy changed. It was the era of the Plowden Report (and a certain amount of hype) and suddenly British primary schools practising discovery-learning, integrated, cross-curricular and child-focused teaching, were world famous. Although not all that was written about British primary schools in the 1970s was true, there is no doubt that changes took place and that primary education did broaden and open out. None of this could have happened if the eleven-plus had still been in existence.

What did happen, around 1978, was that many LEAs re-introduced standardised testing programmes. Circular 10/65, which heralded the introduction of comprehensive schools, had been followed by a dramatic drop in attainment testing in LEAs, but in 1975 and 1977 came the Black Papers with a concern over standards of teaching and learning, and in 1976 James Callaghan, then Prime Minister, made his Ruskin College speech demanding more accountability in education. At this point many LEAs, concerned that they had no information on standards of performance in their primary schools, brought back reading, maths and to a lesser extent verbal reasoning tests. With the time lag that is inevitable in the introduction of testing programmes, it was 1978 that was the key year for the introduction of these new schemes. However, this testing was of little significance: results were not published, there was no competition among schools to do well, there was little link with the curriculum taught and little effect on children's life chances. The results were collected routinely for administrative purposes and as a safety net for the LEA.

Thus, by contrast with the eleven-plus, they had little impact on teaching and their introduction took place alongside the continued expansion of teaching methods and organisation.

National curriculum assessment

How could we characterise British primary education in the late 1980s, post eleven-plus, so that we can consider the impact of national curriculum assessment? It is clear that there is no such thing as a typical primary school, and that descriptive dichotomies such as traditional–progressive, formal–informal, didactic–discovery are too simplistic.

We do know, however, that, despite the failure of the 'Plowden approach' to 'revolutionise' many primary schools, they are quite different places from the days of the eleven-plus. What we can do, therefore, is identify some generalisable characteristics that seem to be common to primary schools today and would have been uncommon 20 years ago. These are:

- mixed ability classes;
- little overt competition among children;
- a certain informality in the relationship between teacher and child;
- a variety of teaching and learning approaches;
- the integration of some subjects into topic work.

National curriculum assessment for Key Stage 1 is upon us and for Key Stage 2 is close behind. At the time of writing, the national tests – standard assessment tasks (SATs) – which form the summative external assessment at the end of the primary key stages (i.e. at 7 and 11) are not yet available, but the plan for Key Stage 1 is that they will be small group and individual tasks or activities for children to carry out. Children will be assessed on the basis of how they perform these tasks. The TGAT Report suggested that they be cross-curricular and could build on from topic work, and that they have practical and oral as well as written elements. All this sounds very different from the eleven-plus, much more open, active and in line with current primary practice. The SATs are being designed like this so that two of the characteristics of primary education listed above – a variety of teaching and learning approaches, and the integration of some subjects into topic work – can continue. This is to be welcomed, since if the SATs were more like traditional exams or the eleven-plus, the backwash effect would force a return to more traditional didactic teaching of separate subjects with the emphasis on written work.

The other element of national assessment is continuous teacher assessment against the statements of attainment. This is essentially for formative purposes, so that the teacher can assess, record, plan and modify the child's teaching programme. Teachers already do this but usually in a less formal way, often keeping their assessment in their head. Provided teachers get some guidance and preparation for this formative part of national curriculum assessment, it could be most valuable. The detailed assessment information which results will form the basis of communication between parent and teacher, and between teacher and teacher within the school.

The amount and type of information which parents will receive about their children's achievements, progress and future work could help enormously in the dialogue between parents and schools.

Another aspect of primary teaching which good formative assessment should help is the 'match' between the child's level of attainment and the task set. As Plowden warned, teachers must '. . . avoid the twin pitfalls of demanding too much and expecting too little' (DES, 1967, para 874). Matching is not a matter of giving children tasks that they can already do; it means providing children with experiences that they can grasp with their existing ideas or skills, but which also demand an extension or modification of present ideas and skills (Harlen, 1982). To provide for this match of experiences to pupils, it is necessary to know what the present ideas and skills of the children are, and this is where assessment comes in. Matching depends on information about children which teachers must gather in the course of day-to-day work, from good formative assessment.

The level of 'match' is something that HMI regularly warn about. In their classic survey of primary schools published in 1978, they reported that, apart from language and maths,

> 'there was a widespread tendency to underestimate the capacities of all groups of children, particularly the more able, in relation to the work they were required to do. If children are to reach satisfactory standards in a full range of work within the curriculum, there is a need to raise the general level of assumptions about what children are capable of doing and to establish sequences of learning in all subjects which will enable children to make progress and have confidence in their own abilities and capacities.' (HMI, 1978, para 6.21)

In a major classroom study following the HMI survey, Bennett and Desforges found that in 16 top infant classes (that is, Y2 in the new terminology) with experienced and able teachers only 40 per cent of tasks were adequately matched. The situation for the more able children was again particularly disturbing: they were underestimated on 41 per cent of all tasks assigned to them. Bennett and

Desforges concluded that at top infants, the level of match was less good in core areas of the curriculum than HMI had found at junior level (Bennett *et al*, 1984). It is extremely difficult to get the match right for 25–30 children within mixed ability classes in an unstructured system; regular assessment against detailed statements of attainment should help teachers here.

Grouping practices are likely to change under the new arrangements. The national curriculum assessment system of 'age-free' levels allows for progression, while also accommodating differentiation. This age-free level system has much in common with graded assessment schemes, notably the idea that children work through at their own pace. One of the problems with graded assessment schemes is that of grouping children who are working at different levels, and this was identified early on as likely to be an issue in national curriculum assessment.

Circular no. 3 from the National Curriculum Council (NCC) on implementing the national curriculum in primary schools says 'the organisation of classes by age may not in all cases be the most effective' (NCC, 1989), which suggests a move towards grouping by level rather than age. This has already been put forward by the Director of Education for Wandsworth (one of the new education authorities created by the break up of the ILEA), as the basis on which children in primary schools will be grouped. This, of course, is not the same as streaming, which involves children of the same age being divided up into separate groups on the basis of ability. It suggests an organisation in which children of different ages but similar levels of attainment are grouped together. It also differs from vertical grouping in that level of attainment is the feature on which children are grouped and sorted.

Perhaps Level One and Level Two will replace Infant One, Infant Two and so on. We have not had a system of grouping like this in our schools for many years (when we had Standard One, Standard Two), so we do not know what it will be like, but we can predict two things: first, more able children will go through the levels, and therefore teaching groups more quickly, and second, the groups will contain younger, more able children with older, less able children.

It seems unlikely that we will get the extremes of bright six-year-olds in with less able eleven-year-olds – few people would think that this was appropriate for their social and emotional development – but certainly rigid age grouping seems to have had its day.

There is another element of national assessment which will have a profound effect on primary schools. This relates to the aggregated summative information which must be published at 11 and may be published at 7. Whether published at 7 or not, it must be made available to parents, governors and the LEA at both ages (not for individual children, of course, but for age groups and classes).

This aggregated *summative* information has quite a different purpose from the formative assessment and will, therefore, have a different impact. This aggregated published data is there to enable competition and comparison. If the data were not to be published, it would not need to be aggregated and children assigned to a level for each subject.

There can be little doubt about the competitive element. The red document, *National Curriculum: From Policy to Practice*, says 'LEAs will *not* be *required* to publish 'league tables' for the schools in their area' (DES, 1989a, para 7.4) (their emphasis) and '. . . making available rank orders for pupils in a class will not be mandatory'. But it will be allowed. This sort of listing and competition will work its way down towards the classroom, and more formal competition will become evident among children.

I am not suggesting that children in primary schools are not competitive now, they are; they often know who is best at maths or reading. They, and their parents, use whatever evidence comes to hand to make these judgements, whether it is progress through the reading scheme or the number of stars on the tables chart. But the national assessment system will result in competitiveness of a different kind and degree. Indeed, the assessment system is designed to enable and encourage comparison. This will result in competitiveness of a completely different order from that inspired by reading schemes.

At the moment children can get to the end of primary schooling without ever having failed an exam, and certainly without feeling they are failures or 'second-rate'. Under the new system this seems most unlikely to continue (leaving aside the rhetoric of differentiation, which allows every child to show what they can do). More likely is a return to competitiveness and an emphasis on individual effort. Competitiveness is a definite feature of the European system. As Chisholm points out (1987),

> 'pupils [in Germany] are under great pressure to achieve demonstrably and continuously. Equally significant is the process of internal socialisation in the primary school years, whereby children gradually learn to see grading as personal affirmation'.

Children who are able and confident will no doubt flourish in the new system, as in the old, but what about the self-image of the less able children? To encourage them to come to terms with their level of ability at a very much younger age than hitherto means that the real world will enter the world of the primary school. My firm belief is that part of the role of the primary school is to protect the young child from the real world, while he or she develops at his or her own pace within a secure, supportive environment; this will be much more difficult to achieve within a competitive system. Mr Baker, the architect of the national curriculum, however, was not concerned about this argument; he is quoted as saying: '"It has become rather unfashionable to give tests to children today because there is the belief that that segregated the winners from the losers" . . . Parents knew such an approach was bogus' (*Daily Telegraph*, 9 February 1987).

Perhaps the vast amount of standardised test material sold by NFER-Nelson only went to unfashionable schools. The point Mr Baker missed is that it is not the giving of tests that causes concern, but the use of the results. Used professionally and privately to promote the education of individual children they can rarely do harm. When used to encourage competition and comparison, and to force market pressure on to schools, there is much more reason to be concerned.

Whether the easy informality which characterises many primary classrooms becomes strained as teachers move into a formal assessment role, we cannot yet say. The re-emergence of more formal relationships may, of course, be popular with many parents who will recognise the formality and discipline of their own school days.

To sum up, it looks as though, of the five characteristics of today's primary schools that were listed earlier in this chapter, two – mixed ability teaching and little overt competition – are likely to change in the wake of national curriculum assessment; two more – a variety of teaching and learning approaches and the integration of subjects into topic work – will not change *if* the SATs are able to encompass these approaches. As for the fifth – the easy informality between teacher and child – we shall have to wait and see whether national curriculum assessment has an effect on this.

7

Graded Assessment

In this chapter we are going to look at a fairly new type of assessment—graded assessment. Many secondary teachers are already familiar with this approach in modern languages and maths; primary teachers are probably much less so. Though graded assessment is not widely used at primary level it is important for primary teachers to understand it for this is the model, more than any other, on which national assessment is based.

Definitions

Graded tests (e.g. in modern languages) are essentially tests which relate to a *series* of teaching objectives in increasing order of difficulty, each one building on from the previous one. Children work their way through them, taking the tests when they are ready to pass. The tests relate directly to the taught material, which is grouped into shorter periods of study than is usual—particularly in, for example, the two-year GCSE course. Graded assessments (e.g. in maths) use the same underlying model, but with more flexibility in progression and assessment procedures. However the terms are often used interchangeably. For the purposes of this chapter I shall use the term graded assessment to include both graded tests and graded assessments.

A recent study of the impact of graded tests identifies three features that are common to most schemes: level-progression, success-orientation and curriculum-linking (Pennycuick and Murphy, 1988).

Level-progression means that there is a sequence of objectives at progressive levels of difficulty, complexity or syllabus content. This involves organising the subject matter into a series of stages, with each one building on the next. This exercise is considered to be easier for subjects such as maths, in which a hierarchical system can easily be seen, than for subjects such as history and geography. Not every pupil must start at the bottom, nor follow the progression absolutely, and within a grade level there can be flexibility in the order of treatment of topics. In some schemes flexibility between different grade levels is also encouraged, so that pupils can be taking assessments across a range of levels at any one time. Some levels may be by-passed as far as assessment is concerned if each level is assumed to subsume previous levels. The same assessment task can also be used for more than one grade level, improved performance being the differentiating factor.

Basically 'graded' in graded assessment means that students get a series of certificates for successive grades, i.e. it refers to the grading of the assessments themselves rather than the grading of pupil performance, as, for example, grading within GCSE (Harrison, 1982).

Success-orientation involves pupils being entered for the assessment when they are likely to pass. This is possible since what constitutes successful performance is predetermined. In other words, it is a criterion-referenced assessment with the criteria for each grade clearly specified, rather than norm-referenced assessment with certain percentages of candidates passing. In this sense the tests are non-competitive and any child who fails can try again. However, the point is to *avoid* failure, which means being flexible about the timing of entering pupils for assessment (which we shall explore later). A corollary of this success orientation is intended to be improved motivation: by avoiding failure, pupils will have a more positive attitude towards the work, and success at one level will encourage the child to work hard for the next level, which will not be too far away.

Curriculum-linking is a key feature in graded assessment, the idea being to specify clearly exactly what will be taught and tested. This specification is made clear to the pupil so that he or she knows what is required, and there is no attempt to 'catch the pupil out' in the assessments. The specification is also made clear on the certificate so that parents and employers know what the student has learnt. This specification normally takes the shape of objectives for teaching and learning.

We can begin to see now how the national curriculum assessments fit into the graded assessment model. The statements of attainment are the objectives which must be taught and against which children are assessed; the ten levels in national curriculum assessment are the progressive levels through which children must go; success orientation is less clear, but within the TGAT scheme the idea is that children go through the levels at their own pace and are assessed at 7, 11, 14 and 16 at their own appropriate level rather than at some pre-determined level—there is therefore an element of success orientation. The link between national curriculum assessment and graded assessment does not have to be argued: Professor Paul Black, the TGAT chairman, who has been involved in the development of graded assessment in science, is on record as saying that graded assessment schemes are the closest of all to the TGAT model (*TES*, 14 July, 89, p. 11).

Another element of some graded assessments, according to one of their proponents, is the close link possible between the assessment and teaching. Thus the assessment can be used diagnostically to determine or modify the child's teaching programme (Brown, 1983). This of course is the ultimate in formative assessment, and is one of the ways in which the teacher assessment element of national curriculum assessment is supposed to operate.

The background to graded assessment

It is interesting to look at why graded assessment developed. The point made in chapter 1 about new techniques not developing in a vacuum, but in response to some need or for a particular purpose, is well illustrated here.

The graded test movement started in modern languages in the mid 1970s. (Harrison, *op cit*). This was largely due to dissatisfaction with traditional methods of teaching *and* assessing modern languages. These had been reasonably appropriate for grammar school pupils, but with the advent of comprehensive schools and the resulting increase in the number and range of pupils exposed to second-language teaching, it became clear that many pupils were finding the subject dull, irrelevant and de-motivating. In order to keep modern languages on the timetable a new approach had to be found.

The Graded Objectives in Modern Languages (GOML) schemes thus had a two-pronged approach: first, a communicative approach to the language, which emphasised speaking and listening rather than written work; second they offered graded tests, with short self-contained units of study and success at the (near) end rather than some (seemingly endless) four-year course leading to O-level/ CSE, with a high probability of failure. The GOML movement was remarkably successful: by 1985 there were 88 groups developing

GOML schemes, with over 300,000 pupils involved (Pennycuick and Murphy, *op cit*).

Then in 1982 the Cockroft Report on Mathematics (DES, 1982) recommended the development of what they called 'graduated tests' in maths for low attainers. This suggestion, that graded tests be for the lower end of the ability range, is one that stemmed from the view that it is this group of pupils who find it most difficult to maintain motivation through a one- or two-year course with limited chance of success at the end. However, there was concern that this would lead to a divisive situation in schools between low and high attainers, potentially more divisive than the O-level/CSE split (Mortimore, 1983).

There was, however, a graded test scheme in maths being developed in Kent as early as 1970. This is a task-based individualised learning and assessment programme. There are nine levels: Level One is that of an average 10-year-old level, Level Nine is slightly above the old O-level standard. Pupils work at their own pace through a set or matrix of tasks (workcards, tapes or booklets) and at the end of the set they take a test. On the basis of how the pupil performs in the test, the teacher makes the choice of tasks within the next matrix. Pupils in the class are therefore working at different levels and the teacher's role is diagnostic and tutorial (Kent Mathematics Project, 1978). It is a popular and well established scheme currently used by a large number of primary and secondary schools in Kent and in other LEAs. The SMILE scheme which is used in many London schools is an adaptation of the Kent Mathematics Project.

One outcome of the Cockroft Report's suggestion was the funding of the Lower Attaining Maths Project, which developed graded tests for secondary pupils. It is now called the Raising Achievement in Maths Project, based in Sussex, East Anglia and Cambridgeshire, and focuses on primary aged children.

The Hargreaves Report on Improving Secondary Schools (ILEA, 1984) came out firmly in favour of the development of graded tests/assessment in maths, English, modern languages, science and CDT. Alongside them, it elaborated a system of units and credits, i.e. six- to eight-week learning units with clear, tangible assessments at the end. The credit '. . . will, we believe, enhance pupil motivation for the unit as well as for the succeeding units . . .'.

Following on from this, the University of London School Examinations Board (ULSEB) developed graded tests, in conjunction with the ILEA and Kent, in both Urdu and French. The Urdu assessments have a culture and literature section as well as a language section, since they are aimed primarily at children whose first language is Urdu.

Work on progressive assessments in science began in 1972 at secondary level and there are a number of sciences schemes available, including the Graded Assessment in Science Project (GASP) within the ULSEB/ILEA/Kent consortium, and the Avon School Science Certificate which is described in Pennycuick and Murphy (1988, *op cit*).

Issues

There are three issues related to graded assessment; these are: motivation, organisation and readiness.

Pupil motivation is the reason most often given for the development and use of graded assessment. The motivating potential is related to the emphasis on success. In traditional exams, many pupils are faced with tasks at an inappropriate level of difficulty and, in the case of norm-referencing, are compared unfavourably with others (Pennycuick and Murphy, *op cit*). It seems quite apparent that by waiting until pupils are ready to pass (i.e. the assessments are appropriate) and by viewing passing in terms of competing against oneself, getting certificates and acquiring skills rather than competing against others, that pupils, particularly those who are not academically able, have a better chance of generating and maintaining enthusiasm for the work.

In a survey of GOML schemes in 1981, Harrison found that pupil motivation and/or enthusiasm was by far the most frequently mentioned successful feature of these schemes (Harrison, 1982, *op cit*). An HMI survey of graded tests in modern languages in Leeds found that they had indeed improved the motivation of some pupils: 'Pupils like to receive certificates and parents are pleased when their children are presented with them' (*TES*, 2 August, 1985). A survey of GOML teaching in Northern Ireland found that the promise of a certificate after each graded test was seen to motivate the less able (McEwan *et al*, 1988).

It is obviously important that the targets or levels should be attainable in order to promote success, but, Pennycuick and Murphy argue, this success must also be *valid*, i.e. passing the graded test must be synonymous with acquiring the tested skills. If it is not, pupil perception of success may be short-lived, since they will be able to 'see through' the value of the certificate (as may others, and it is important to the notion of success that others perceive the success too).

The receiving of certificates relates to external or extrinsic motivation which may well drop off if lower attaining pupils see everyone in the class receiving them too—perhaps many more certificates than they do. However, with the advent of national curriculum assessment we are unlikely to be in a situation where children will be exposed to a range of graded tests with certificates for all subjects. For although national curriculum assessment is on the graded assessment model, it is not envisaged that it will involve short units of work and certificates. A warning point to make about certification is that, although graded assessment can be seen as non-competitive, nevertheless some children will progress further and faster than others: 'All children pass, but some are definitely more passing than others' (Richmond, 1984). It will still be evident that some children are more successful than others.

Intrinsic motivation is more likely to increase as a result of changes in curriculum or pedagogy associated with the graded assessment scheme rather than the graded assessment itself. For example, the communicative approach to learning in the GOML schemes has improved pupil motivation because pupils like this approach and can see its relevance. So these schemes are popular because the student can succeed *and* because he or she can see the value of the activity. For example, the Northern Ireland study mentioned earlier found that pupils after three terms of GOML found French more fun than those taught by other methods, and boys in mixed schools saw French as relevant and *not* as a 'cissy' subject. Of course another important factor in motivating pupils is teacher enthusiasm and this is likely to be more in evidence with new developments, particularly ones emanating from local groups as with the GOML schemes.

Clearly then, not all the motivating potential of graded assessment comes from the assessment itself. One of the elements that contributes to motivation is that pupils take the assessments when ready to pass. The principle of 'readiness' is crucial to the success-orientation of graded assessment. What could be worse for motivation than to take regular tests and assessments and to keep failing them?

This is not always easy to achieve, however, partly because teachers may find it difficult to know when particular children are ready, and partly because it can be difficult to organise the testing of children at different times. The 1984 HMI survey of graded tests in modern languages in Leeds, referred to earlier, found that the readiness principle was *not* operated in French at secondary level: pupils were entered as a group and pass rates were correspondingly lower than expected—about 50 per cent rather than the 80 per cent which is common in mastery learning schemes. 'Entering pupils for the tests at the appropriate moment so that they are more likely to be successful is a better way of improving motivation than entry in lock-step because high failure rates in French are not likely to be motivating' (*TES*, 2 August, 1985).

Graded tests in music and other performing arts are held three or four times a year on fixed dates, so that flexibility in entry is possible. In the Kent Mathematics Project (KMP) work is individualised and testing is an integral part of the course, thus entry decisions are not taken as such. What happens is that students reach an assessment and take it within their individual work programme. In the GOML schemes, however, this is more difficult since assessment is not incorporated into a planned learning sequence. What often happens is that a level is planned to cover a year's work and the level tests are given as end-of-year examinations. Inevitably therefore some pupils are not ready when the assessment is done, while others are ready some time before. Not only does testing the whole class together make organisation easier, it reduces the amount of time spent in testing, which is an important feature where tests are given by teachers. However, testing the whole class or group together does jeopardise the motivating potential and success orientation for many pupils. Many of the maths schemes avoid this issue because assessments are self-administered; there is an advantage here, apparently, in that where pupils decide for themselves when they have mastered objectives and are ready for the assessment the element of self-assessment can be motivating.

The issue of readiness is clearly related to the organisation of classrooms. Pennycuick and Murphy (1986) offer six strategies to enable the principle of readiness to operate:

1. Providing extra work for slow learners, outside class time, to enable them to keep up;
2. Allowing the class to go at the speed of its slower members and offering the faster students extension work or allowing them to help the slower one;
3. Going for fully individualised programmes of study, as in some of the maths schemes;
4. Reorganising the allocation of pupils to classes so that grouping is by mixed age rather than mixed ability *and* allowing sufficient flexibility so that pupils can change classes as they succeed at a level;
5. Designing assessments which are sufficiently skills-based to be virtually content-free (though they do not say how). Tests can then be independent of the course material taught and can be added on to existing class-based teaching programmes;
6. If levels in a scheme subsume previous ones, a course can be taught to a class which covers all the objectives for, say, three levels. At the end of the year children can be assessed at whichever level they have reached.

The third of these strategies is quite widely used, but would not be appropriate if extended to a range of subjects. Reorganising by level rather than by age is a possibility which has been put forward by the National Curriculum Council (NCC), among others, in order to facilitate national curriculum assessment (NCC, 1989, *op cit*), though flexibility will still be a problem. The last strategy is also a possibility and one that is advocated by a number of graded assessment schemes at present.

Another issue related to flexible timing of assessments is that of test security and availability. If flexibility is required, all the assessments will have to be made available near the start of the year and this does raise questions about security, teaching to the test, etc, since it goes very much against traditional notions of unseen, external (and therefore high status) examination.

Clearly, using flexible graded assessment requires considerable expertise on behalf of the teacher in relation to match, diagnostic assessment, organisation and resource management.

A critique of graded assessment

As well as these essentially practical issues, there are some more fundamental critiques of graded assessment.

First, in schemes in which mastery of one level is essential before moving on to the next, passing an assessment inappropriately (i.e. when the pupil should have failed) could have serious implications (Nuttall and Goldstein, 1984). Indeed it could be as damaging as if a pupil failed an assessment and was denied the opportunity to move up a level when ready. This, of course, is little different from the effects of students wrongly passing and failing ordinary exams.

Second, the question arises whether progression from one level or grade to the next is appropriate for all subjects. Most subjects are taught on a principle of progress in terms of increasing difficulty and complexity of tasks, but without there being assumed to be an underlying progression of difficulty of objectives. In subjects such as history and geography, there will be a number of possible routes through the syllabus and mastering one section of the syllabus may not be essential before moving on to the next. In a non-hierarchical subject, then, the sections of study or levels need not be arranged in any particular order; this means that they involve not necessarily *graded* tests but possibly *modular* tests: 'tests on self-contained content that can be taken in any order and whose material can be forgotten without apparent penalty after the test has been taken' (Nuttall and Goldstein, 1984, *op cit*).

Even in mathematics, though, which some see as a subject which is clearly hierarchically-ordered there is some disagreement over whether this is the case. For example there is some criticism (Noss *et al*, 1989) of the hierarchical ordering underpinning the Graded Assessment in Mathematics (GAIM) scheme which was the first graded assessment scheme to be made equivalent to GCSE. The argument of Noss and colleagues is that the use of the term 'hierarchy' denotes a series of stages representing some natural pattern of learning; they do not believe that such 'universal necessary stages' exist even in the learning of mathematics. The response of the developers of GAIM is that they believe there are *local* hierarchies within conceptual areas of maths (e.g. multiplication is more difficult for a learner than addition) and that development can proceed at different rates within these areas, but that their empirical evidence indicates that the GAIM levels are an adequate approximation to children's learning (Brown, 1989).

The third issue is to do with the descriptions on certificates of what pupils are able to do at each level or grade, and the importance of context and specificity in these descriptions. The questions at issue here are, can descriptions of skills be context-free and how reliable are loosely worded descriptions? To take an extreme case, the more precise a statement or description is in terms of definition *and* context, the more clear we are that the pupil can or cannot do the specified task or level. But this will lead to many, detailed statements. If we wish to reduce the number of statements, the definitions must become looser and context-free and further away from the assessments. We are then less certain that a student who has passed the test, or reached that level, can do the things specified on the certificate.

An example to illustrate this point is taken from GOALS (Graded Objectives for Achievement in Language Skills). A Level One skill is 'can buy food and drink in a cafe'. What we do not know is whether the child who has reached this level can do this in a real French cafe or only in the simulated one at school, and what sort of range of items he or she can buy (Pennycuick and Murphy, 1988 *op cit*). However, the more specific the descriptions become, the more context-bound and detailed they also become, thus making the assessments too many and too detailed, with the risk of assessment overloading the teaching. Having a comprehensive list of items of food and drink which the pupil should be able to buy would make the assessment much more time consuming, and yet one would have a much clearer idea of what the child could and could not order.

We know also that context is very important to performance, the APU's work having shown, for example, that addition tasks are easier when set out vertically than horizontally, and easier if set within a written task that is meaningful to the pupil. This point about context is of course relevant whenever an assessment aims to say what a pupil can do; in other words it is true of all criterion-referenced assessment, of which graded assessment is only one example. GCSE is another example, and the descriptions of what pupils can do (i.e. grade-related criteria) have also been a problem; this will be discussed in detail in the next chapter.

Looking to the future, it is clear that graded assessment has much to offer, as well as some problems. What seems clear, too is that it has a rosy future, since, as already pointed out, national curriculum assessment is to follow this route. The Consortium for Assessment and Testing in Schools (CATS), which received the largest part of the funding for the development of 14+ assessments, has plans which 'reflect the latest developments in the graded assessment scheme where pupils are tested not by a "sudden death" three-hour end-of-course exam, but throughout the course in progressive stages' (*TES*, 14 July, 1989, p. 11). This consortium includes King's College, London, which has been a pioneer in the development of graded assessment. Certainly this is an exciting opportunity to develop new across-the-board assessments in a range of subjects. Issues of flexibility, readiness and organisation will, however, need to be addressed.

8

GCSE: Criterion-Referencing and Differentiation

The GCSE is supposed to be a criterion-referenced examination. As we have seen, 'criterion-referenced' means that performance is reported in relation to well-defined criteria, rather than in relation to the performance of a population of students. The aim in criterion-referenced assessment is to specify what individual students know, understand and can do. One corollary, in theory, is that students will pit themselves against defined levels of achievement rather than compete against each other, so that all students can be successful in their own terms. By indicating levels of achievement across the components or domains of a subject, a profile of achievements can be built up for a student. These profiles can offer motivation to students who might otherwise come into the approximately 40 per cent who would have 'nothing to celebrate and nothing to strive for under a system tied to a norm-referenced system' (McNaughton, 1989).

Whatever happened to grade-related criteria?

However, specifying the criteria in criterion-referenced assessment is not always easy and has proved to be a particular problem in GCSE. Sir Keith Joseph's announcement of the new GCSE in 1984 included a reference to grade-related criteria—the criteria which students would have to meet in order to gain a particular grade:

> 'examination grades should have a clearer meaning and pupils and teachers need clearer goals. We accordingly need grade-related

criteria which will specify the knowledge, understanding and skills expected for the award of particular grades.' (DES, 1987b)

One of the reasons for the interest of the DES and Secondary Examinations Council (SEC) in the development of criterion-referencing within GCSE was concern over comparability, or rather the lack of it, in GCE grades from different boards. With a single, consistent, system of clearly-defined grades, all the exam boards would apply the same standards in awarding grades (Orr and Nuttall, 1983).

There were already grade descriptions in the GCSE subject criteria, developed by the SEC, which gave a broad idea of the performance likely to have been shown by a candidate awarded a particular grade, but what was wanted were more specific descriptions of performance. So the SEC set up working parties in each of the main subjects to develop grade criteria. These working parties first identified 'domains'—coherent and defined areas of knowledge, understanding and skills within each subject (which can be thought of as equivalent to the profile components in national curriculum assessment). The groups then broke the domains down into abilities and produced definitions of performance, or criteria, required for achievement at different levels. These draft grade criteria were then put out for consultation, in 1985. As a result of this consultation exercise the DES conceded two points.

First, the complexity of the draft grade criteria militated against their usefulness, 'particularly to employers' (DES, 1987b, *op cit*). What had happened was that the working parties had produced numerous and often complex criteria which made their assessment unmanageable. In history, for example, there were ten sub-elements across three domains and criteria were given for four levels of performance within each sub-element (and in GCSE there are seven levels, i.e. grades), adding up to 40 statements of performance to be used not only by those doing the assessment but also by those interpreting candidates' performance. In English the problem lay in the rather broad criteria formulated, which made reliable differentiation between performance at different grades very difficult. An example taken from the domain of writing will make this clear: to get a grade A/B a candidate should 'Give a coherent and perceptive account of both actual and imagined experience', while to get a grade F/G he or she should 'Give a coherent account of personal experience'. At the other extreme, the maths group produced eighty detailed criteria for *one domain* at a *single grade* level (Brown, 1988).

Second, the DES recognised that care was needed to make sure that teaching and assessment strategies based on the draft grade criteria would not lead to the breaking down of subjects into isolated tasks. This, of course, is bound to be a danger where there is a highly specified curriculum and/or assessment. The problem for criterion-referenced assessment, as we have already seen with graded assessment, is that the more specific the criteria, the more reliable the assessment is likely to be, but it is burdensome, and the more fragmented teaching is likely to become. The SEC had been aware of this problem for some time (Murphy, 1986b) and in the briefing paper to the draft grade criteria subject working parties said that:

> 'The rigorous specification of full criterion-referencing for assessment in the GCSE would result in very tightly defined syllabuses and patterns of assessment which would not allow the flexibility of approach that characterises education in this country.' (SEC, 1984, p. 2)

In order to refine and develop the draft grade criteria the SEC funded a re-marking exercise. This involved the re-marking of the 1986 joint O-level/CSE exam scripts according to the draft criteria. This exercise threw up a host of problems. First, there was a poor match between the domains and levels produced by the working parties and the content of the exam papers studied; this was not particularly surprising since these exam papers had not been designed to cover the domains and levels. But more importantly, there were ambiguities in the criteria. The hierarchies of performance given by the draft grade criteria bore little relationship to the actual responses of candidates to specific questions. There was a lack of equivalence between the same levels of performance on different questions and across different domains. And, as far as a pilot exam in history based directly on the draft grade criteria was concerned, they demonstrated a real problem in moving from the four levels of performance in draft grade criteria to the seven grades used in GCSE. The report of research carried out by the London East Anglian Group in chemistry and history concluded that the draft grade criteria were largely unworkable (Kingdon and Stobart, 1987).

At this point, the draft grade criteria were dropped. As the DES paper put it: 'In the light of this outcome from the re-marking exercise, the SEC decided to approach from a different angle the task of making GCSE grades more objective.' (DES, 1987b, *op cit*, para 13.)

This new angle involved the development of *performance matrices* which meant starting the other way round, arguably the better way round. The starting point was some of the existing approved GCSE syllabuses and the task was to develop, for these particular syllabuses (which had, of course, to conform to the GCSE general and specific criteria) specific descriptions of performance, 'attributes', at different levels. These attributes defined as 'a quality developed in students who follow a particular course' are described at different levels of performance (e.g. Grades A, C and F) and combined into domains. [Quite how the introduction of the concept of attributes was to help in an already hugely complicated area is not at all clear]. The point about performance matrices is that they relate to individual syllabuses rather than the whole subject, and they are based on examiners' articulation of their implicit judgements in awarding grades.

The final reports of the working parties were produced in mid-1988 with varied reactions to the viability of performance matrices. But when the SEC was superseded by the School Examinations and Assessment Council (SEAC) at the end of 1988 one of the first things it did was to freeze all work on performance matrices. By mid-1989 it reported that it was sponsoring work on performance matrices (SEAC, 1989). In the summer of 1988 however, the first GCSE papers were graded on the basis of the original (loose) grade descriptions, while the proportions of candidates receiving various grades were held roughly constant in line with O-level and CSE. This is, roughly speaking, what has always happened. Public exam grading has always involved the use of some performance criteria, if vague and flexible, used in conjunction with statistical information to determine final cut-off scores for the grades (Christie and Forrest, 1981).

In the summer of 1989 the same approach was used for grading and the percentage of candidates gaining high grades increased marginally: 46.1 per cent received grades A–C compared with 42.5 per cent in 1988 (*Education*, 25 August, 1989). Of course, this cannot *necessarily* be taken to mean higher standards since the grading is *not* against specific criteria.

With the advent of a criterion-referenced national assessment system there seems little point in continuing the search for performance matrices, or grade-related criteria. Both national assessment and GCSE will have to follow the attainment targets for Key Stage 4 and these will form the basis for criterion-referencing. Some of the existing graded assessment schemes will also form the new criterion-referenced basis for assessment at 16-plus.

England is not the first country to find the development of a criterion-referenced national assessment system difficult. Scotland had problems with the 16-plus Standard Grade exam. The aim there, as with GCSE, was to bring about a number of curricular and assessment reforms, one of them being a move towards criterion-referencing. Within each area of the curriculum there were between three and five assessment elements, or domains (e.g. practical skills, communication), and grades were to be given for performance in each element, thus giving a profile of performance. There are seven grades (for which grade-related criteria were developed) differentiated broadly under three levels of certificate examination (credit, general and foundation levels). Thus, within one subject, a student could follow a course at one of three levels and a Standard Grade Certificate could be awarded at one of seven grades on four elements; as well as the exam, teachers may have had to assess pupils within all of these and in any combination. Also, teachers had to submit estimated grades for each pupil in each element on a 19-point scale, whereas under the old Ordinary Grade they simply had to produce an order of merit on a whole course basis, and give marks for any internally assessed component.

As a result of the concern felt by many teachers over this new system, a committee was set up under the chairmanship of Dr E. McClelland, HM Chief Inspector for Scotland, in October 1985 to 'consider the scope for simplification' of the assessment. The Committee was popularly known as the 'Simple Committee' and it did indeed recommend a number of simplifications.

Among these was a reduction in the number of elements (or domains) assessed; that continuous assessment be for feedback to teachers rather than for certification; that the grade-related criteria be defined only for three of the six levels of performance (the seventh grade simply indicates completion of the course); that the grade-related criteria be used to help teachers plan courses rather than used in assessment of the many tasks and exercises undertaken by pupils; and that estimated grades be submitted on a seven-point scale per element rather than nineteen (Gipps, 1986).

The message from the Scottish experience, which seems to have been ignored by the DES, ministers and SEAC, is that a system which is too complex will not be feasible.

We have already looked at two problems in criterion-referencing in GCSE: the difficulty of finding the language to describe criteria which allows differentiation among them, and the complexity for both assessor and user of assessments if a large number of criteria is envisaged. But there is a third problem and that is to do with aggregation, i.e. the 'collapsing' of the detailed performance profile for each individual into a single reporting figure, or grade.

Aggregating the detailed assessment information into a crude single grade compromises the motivating potential of criterion-referencing. If the candidate is not given feedback on his or her detailed performance profile how can the performance profile improve motivation, and indeed why have the complex structure of domains, etc, in the first place? A final summative aggregated grade does not help the employer much either: it obscures more than it clarifies. If an exam assesses five domains, elements or components, candidates with a high overall grade may have done well on (any) three or four and poorly on the other(s). The high grade therefore tells us little about what the pupil is capable of doing (Scott, 1989). It is not likely therefore that GCSE examination grades will have more meaning for employers. This is a clear example of the summative or reporting role overwhelming the formative role in assessment.

It must be clear by now that many of these issues are highly pertinent to national curriculum assessment, and we will pick them up again in the next chapter.

Differentiation in GCSE

Another feature of GCSE is the concept of differentiation. During the trials and pilot work to develop a common exam at 16-plus, there was concern about the technical difficulties involved in examining over a wide range of abilities (Schools Council, 1971). The Waddell Committee, which was set up to oversee an independent study of the joint 16-plus exam, favoured a common exam in some subjects but argued that in certain subjects (e.g. maths and modern languages), where the range of skills was wide or where certain concepts might be beyond the reach of many candidates, a range of papers would be needed. These *differentiated papers*, as they were called, would be needed to allow all candidates to show what they could do, and to allow the inclusion of items suitable for some candidates only, without distorting the curriculum for others (DES, 1978a). These suggestions were incorporated into a White Paper which recommended that 'alternative papers are used wherever necessary to maintain standards' (DES, 1978b).

This notion put forward in the Waddell Report, of allowing all candidates to show what they can do, is the forerunner to the notion of 'positive achievement' in GCSE. The need to allow all candidates to show what they could do was, over the next seven years, developed into the concept of positive achievement with its overtones of motivating potential. Positive achievement, linked to differentiation, became increasingly important in the rhetoric of GCSE. As the new exam became a reality, Sir Keith Joseph talked about, and the DES wrote about, pitching papers and questions at different levels of difficulty so allowing all pupils 'to show what they know, understand and can do' (DES, 1985). The SEC stressed that assessment should be a positive experience for all rather than a dispiriting one, and therefore candidates should not be presented with tasks that were too difficult (SEC, 1985). If assessment was a positive experience, the argument went, motivation would be enhanced.

The national subject criteria for GCSE then stipulated that for maths, modern languages, physics, chemistry, biology, science and business studies, differentiation must be achieved by candidates sitting different exam papers leading to different grades. The exam boards developed three main models of differentiated exams: the three-in-line model, the four overlapping papers model, and the extension papers model.

The three-in-line model (also called the Alternative Papers model) consists of one common paper and a choice of an easier or harder second paper. The easier route offers grades G to C and the harder route grades A to D (usually); if candidates for the harder paper do not reach grade D they are Ungraded.

The four overlapping papers model requires candidates to take any adjacent pair of increasingly difficult papers. This results in three routes: the easier route offers grades E (or D) to G, the intermediate route grades C to E (or F), and the harder route offers A to D. Candidates who miss the minimum grade on the latter two routes are Ungraded. This model is almost universally used for maths, since the national criteria for maths state that there will normally be no common paper taken by all candidates.

The extension papers model consists of basic or general (i.e. common) paper(s) with an optional extension paper(s). Grades G to C are available on the basic papers; grades A and B can be reached by taking the extension paper(s). There is no ungraded 'penalty' for doing badly on the extension paper. This model is used for modern languages (with four basic and four extended papers) and increasingly for science syllabuses.

The three-in-line model has two technical problems (Stobart, 1987). The first relates to increments of difficulty: the assumption is that there will be equivalent increments of difficulty from the easier alternative to the common paper and from the common paper to the harder alternative. In fact, in the early years the common paper was at the same level or easier than the easy alternative paper, while the harder alternative paper was harder than the common paper, as expected. Because the 'easy' alternative paper was too hard, it limited the weaker candidates' ability to show what they could do, i.e. to demonstrate positive achievement. The second issue is the equivalence of grades—there was some evidence that where a grade was obtainable via two routes, it was slightly easier to reach it via the easier route than via the harder route (Good and Cresswell, 1988).

With the four overlapping papers model, there were also uneven increments of difficulty across the papers. Papers two and three were of very similar levels of difficulty, paper one was considerably easier than paper two, while the incline of difficulty from paper three to paper four was the only one to be pitched correctly (Stobart, 1987 *op cit*). If papers are not in an evenly ascending order of difficulty then of course this has serious implications for choosing the appropriate pair of papers for candidates to enter. Again there was evidence that it was easier to obtain some grades via easier routes.

For the extension paper model, which does not involve an ungraded penalty result, the choice of paper to be taken is not as crucial. There are, however, critical decisions to be taken by the examiners, notably what score a candidate must get on the common paper before being able to get credit from the extension paper. If the extension and common papers test different skills it is perfectly possible for candidates to do well on the extension paper but fail to reach the cut-off point on the common paper which would allow their score on the extension paper to count. Wherever the hurdle or cut-off point is set, those candidates who pass it and get credit for the extended paper have a chance to improve their grade, so the setting of the cut-off point is very important.

A research study funded by the SEC at the Southern Examining Group looked at teachers' ability to predict students' grades and so to enter them appropriately for differentiated papers. It found that teachers were as successful at predicting grades in January as they were in May (which is when decisions on entry are commonly made). Eighty-five per cent of teachers' predictions were accurate to plus or minus one grade. The report recommended, however, that the grade ranges for different routes be wide enough to give a safety margin, or overlap, of two grades (Good and Cresswell, 1988, *op cit*). They cited evidence from the Southern Examining Group's statistics for its joint exams in 1986 – which showed that 20 per cent of the candidates entered for the highest level in maths were ungraded, as were 13 per cent of those entered for the middle level – to suggest that teachers' entry decisions may be affected by the constraints of the *actual* exam situation (parental pressure, etc). In the research study, teachers were making good entry decisions in an experimental context, while in the real situation a two-grade overlap may be necessary to prevent students being wrongly entered and therefore ungraded.

Clearly, there are technical problems with each of the three models described here, which it is important to overcome if fairness and equity are to be observed.

One of the early concerns about differentiation was that it would be divisive; that in effect the exam would be little different from the old O-level and CSE:

'differentiation means that the system will still be divisive: that there
will be separate routes to the examination; that some candidates will
not be eligible for higher grades (if they take the less difficult route);
that teachers will still have to decide which students are suited for
which route/course/range of grades; that in some cases these decisions will still have to be made as early as fourteen'. (Gipps, 1986, *op
cit*).

A small research study was carried out in order to see whether
these concerns, in particular the last, were justified. It involved
analysing 170 questionnaires returned to an exam board by heads of
department and teachers of maths, physics and French. These
subjects were chosen because they used differentiated papers and
covered the three models described above. The questionnaires
focused on the organisation of teaching groups during the two-year
GCSE course. In addition, during the school year 1987/88, a case
study of the impact of differentiation in a comprehensive school was
carried out. Over the course of the year, staff in the maths, physics,
French and history departments were interviewed, as well as the
examinations officer and two groups of students (19 altogether) just
before they took the exams in May (Gipps, 1988b).

What emerged from this research was that the prediction about
selection for easier or harder routes being made as early as 14, was
quite wrong, and that the system was not as divisive as O-level/CSE.
The realisation that this was a common examining *system* rather
than a common exam was nevertheless slow to dawn on students
and many teachers.

The timing of the selection for papers to be taken was, as a rule,
left until quite late (January in the 5th year) with the mock exams
acting as a crucial factor in the decision. Of the 87 schools returning
questionnaires[1] between a half and three-quarters made the selection after the mocks in French, maths and physics, on the basis of
performance in this exam and performance over the course. In
maths, four schools (11 per cent) selected at the end of the 3rd year
and three (8 per cent) at the end of the 4th year; none of the schools
selected students for their French or physics papers as early as this.
(A handful of schools, all of them independent schools, indicated
that selection was not an issue, since *all* students would be entered
for the higher papers). In maths, the choice of papers was likely to
be pre-empted by the student's set. Despite the emphasis on the
mock exams, teachers 'knew' before this which level the various
students were capable of taking. The mocks were used as a final
piece of information and as a way of showing students themselves

---

[1] I am most grateful to Gordon Stobart and Susan Atkins of ULSEB who allowed me access
to the questionnaires and answered my numerous queries on them.

and their parents which level they should attempt. In all three subjects, movement was possible after the mocks.

These findings were duplicated in the case-study school where final allocation was made after mocks, some movement across papers was made in response to parental pressure or unexpected performance in the mocks, and movement across sets was feasible: 'The problem with CSE and O-level was that the syllabuses were so different you couldn't switch, now it's not a problem, they're all doing the same thing' (Head of French).

The other important issue relating to differentiation is its effect on motivation, through its link with positive achievement. The claim that GCSE will increase motivation through positive achievement is compelling, but needs to be analysed. Similar claims, as we have seen, are made for graded assessment and profiling, but these claims address only extrinsic motivation – that is motivation resulting from the desire to get higher grades – as opposed to intrinsic motivation which results from students' interest or involvement in the learning task and material. Of course, changes in content or teaching style in GCSE may affect intrinsic motivation and there is some preliminary evidence that this has indeed happened (HMI, 1988).

Continuous assessment through coursework is also suggested as having motivating potential. However, teachers face a dilemma, as a study by Taylor and Wallace shows (1988), over how to deal with feedback for students whose grades in GCSE-equivalent terms would be low, and the long term impact of such feedback on motivation to complete the GCSE course. Giving feedback in terms of inflated grades in order to sustain optimism and motivation, a solution adopted by some teachers in the study, would seem to raise as many problems as it solves. Taylor and Wallace suggest dealing with the issue by distinguishing the intermediate tasks and their marking from the long term GCSE goal.

There are two aspects of the differentiation that could adversely affect motivation. One is the limit on grades: students taking basic, foundation or intermediate papers/routes, no matter how hard they try or how well they do, cannot get higher than a specified grade. The other is the chance of being ungraded on the higher or intermediate papers. Both of these aspects could undermine the motivating potential of GCSE.

None of the teachers who completed the questionnaire or were interviewed in the research liked the models of differentiation with a penalty, and there was a dilemma over whether to be cautious over level of entry. By contrast, where there was no penalty (on the extension model) the tendency was to be optimistic in making entries.

It was clear from the case study school that, even once the exam course had begun, many pupils and parents were not aware of differentiation and its implications:

> 'It's not much different from O-level and CSE, you've still got to differentiate the kids . . . It's very difficult, I thought the common exam meant we didn't have to do this.' 'We said to parents at the beginning, "It'll be a common course and a common exam", and it isn't.' (Physics teacher)

The evidence from teachers and children showed that there was a feeling of being let down over differentiation: that they *had* expected a common exam and they clearly had not got one. The teachers interviewed felt that while differentiation might be necessary, the differentiated papers with *penalties* were unfair. The overwhelming reaction to the penalty from students was its unfairness, particularly for borderline candidates. Some students admitted that the risk of being ungraded made them work harder, others that it had stopped them taking the harder papers, although they would have liked the chance to do so.

The penalty for 'missing' on the higher papers in maths and physics they definitely regarded as unfair, particularly for those who were likely to get a C: if they did badly on the day they had a chance of getting nothing:

> 'I don't think it's fair because if you put in for the top paper and don't get a C or D, you get the U, that makes you feel like a failure when you could have got a C in a different way, or a D which is better than a U!'
>
> 'Because employers won't take it into consideration—if they see a "U" they'll just think . . . you're thick!'

With regard to the effect of the penalty, and whether it had made them work harder:

> '. . . Work harder, because you know you've got to get a D or above.'
>
> 'It depends on what grade you're going to get. If you think you're going to get an A and you muck up and get a B, it's not going to worry you, but if you're hoping to get a C, but you're not quite sure, then the cut-off is going to be near where you are. But if you think you're going to get a very high grade, it's not going to bother you.'
>
> 'Well it's made you work a bit harder, I suppose.' (Laughter)
>
> 'Yes *I* am.'

Teachers were more likely to think the *limit on grades* was reasonable – on the grounds that students had a certain level of ability and knew it – than were the students themselves. Again, students thought this unfair and for some of those who knew they could not get higher than a C or an E it was de-motivating:

'Well, you don't really mind, but you obviously don't take it so seriously as you would if you were going to take the higher paper.'

'Some people are going in to Maths knowing they can only get a grade E and, people, they just give up.'

'I think it's unfair that some people, they're cut off from having the chance to get the good grades, I mean they're not given the option, they take the easy option, just because they think, "Oh, I won't be able to do the higher papers" and they take the easy option papers, the highest grade is a C and maybe they realise that they could do better than that.'

Some of the students clearly resented not being allowed access to the full range of grades; they felt that they were *not* allowed to show what they could do. The extension papers model was thought to be best of the three models of differentiated exam as far as the students were concerned:

'I think French is best really, because everyone does basic level, then if you want to, if you think you can do it, you can go and do a higher level.'

This small research study indicated that for these teachers and students there was a problem with differentiation and motivation. On the plus side, it became clear that selection was left as late as possible and that movement across sets and assigned levels was, in theory, possible even after mocks.

Despite some publicity about the numbers of candidates getting an ungraded result in GCSE maths, nothing has been done to change the system. In summer 1988 over 14,900 candidates entered for the harder route were ungraded (Cresswell, 1989): these candidates would have expected to get a high grade and in fact got nothing because they were not allowed access to a lower grade. It makes a mockery of the notion of positive motivation and candidates being able to show what they know, understand and can do. SEAC's comment on this was: 'In biology, chemistry and mathematics there was a tendency for too many candidates to be entered at the high level ... major problems were mainly confined to mathematics where some candidates' (over 14,900!) 'entered at the highest level have been ungraded' (SEAC, 1989). In responding to SEAC's report Kenneth Baker (then Secretary of State for Education) at least made the point that if pupils were entered inappropriately for higher level papers their actual attainments should, nevertheless, receive recognition (DES, 1989c).

If differentiation were possible without a stated limit on the grades available from different papers, then the increased motivation that is supposed to come with positive achievement would be more of a reality. Clearly, criterion-referencing is an important ingredient of positive achievement (though not yet available in GCSE), as is the level of question set for less able children, but the limit on grades specifically reduced motivation for some of the students in the study. The penalty, on the other hand, did frighten some students into working harder, but this 'carrot and stick' motivation is hardly in keeping with the philosophy of positive achievement.

Future Plans

Proposals for integrating GCSE with national curriculum assessment have made it clear that GCSE will be the main method of assessment at 16+ but will be reported in terms of national assessment levels. Level 4 will be the minimum level of attainment to get a GCSE certificate (this, by the way, is the level expected of average 11 year olds), while level 10 would be of a higher standard than the traditional GCSE grade A.

Lower attaining pupils who score on levels 1–3 at age 16 will have this reported in their school record (whatever form this takes), but will not get a GCSE certificate. Although GCSE was originally intended to be available to the whole of the age group over the full ability range, this was probably unrealistic. It is now clear that less able pupils will have only their school record while average and more able pupils will have a GCSE certificate as well as their school record. We are thus back with a two-tier assessment system.

9

National Curriculum Assessment: A Critique

We have discussed national curriculum assessment throughout the course of this book where the issues raised were relevant. I now want to look at some points in more detail.

Criterion-referenced assessment

Let's start with an issue raised in the last chapter: criterion-referencing. National assessment is to be a criterion-referenced system; that is clear, and few would disagree that this is better than a norm-referenced system. But we have to recognise the fact that there are problems in developing criterion-referenced assessment systems. As Nuttall points out, there is no country with a working system of differentiated attainment targets that reports attainment in terms of subject grades, or levels (Nuttall, 1987).

The criteria, or statements of attainment, have been relatively easy to develop, as judged by the speed with which the subject working groups have written them. But that is in a sense the easiest part of the job. We do not yet know whether they are in the right order, and some have to be described in more detail to allow informal teacher assessment to take place. The old tension of specificity versus breadth comes to the fore here. We need specificity to allow for assessment, but we need to beware of breaking down knowledge and understanding into bits abstracted from context: school learning is disconnected enough from real life as it is, without fragmenting the decontextualised skills as well (Nuttall, 1989).

With the evidence of the Scottish experience in mind, there is no doubt that the system as it is proposed is unworkable. Think for a moment about the workload for the average top infants teacher. In the spring term she or he will have to assess all the seven-year-old children on 33 attainment targets for English, maths and science. That does not sound too difficult until one remembers that it is not actually the attainment targets but the statements of attainment that children are being assessed against. For each attainment target there are on average three statements of attainment per level. In any class of seven-year-olds there will be children at three of the ten levels of attainment, at least. Let us say that the average primary class is 30 strong. A simple calculation of the number of attainment targets, by the number of statements of attainment, by the levels, by the number of children in the class ($33 \times 3 \times 3 \times 30$) shows that there is a potential pool of 8,910 bits of information for a teacher of seven-year-olds to deal with. And then of course there will be CDT, history and geography, and by age 11 any class could cover four or five levels of attainment, so the number of bits of information will increase. Perhaps what we need is our own Simple Committee.

And then there is aggregation. Aggregation will pull the detailed assessment information together to put each child at a level on each profile component and subject. SEAC has proposed a 'half or more' rule where there are a number of attainment targets, that is, the child must attain level 'n' on half or more of the attainment targets to be deemed to be at level 'n' for that profile component.

Aggregation is inevitable in any assessment system which has to reduce detailed information to simple information for publication. The problem with aggregating on a 'half or more' principle is that it weakens criterion-referencing. If a child is at level 'n' on a profile component or subject, this tells us nothing about what level the child is at on any individual attainment target. It would be more appropriate to require, on mastery learning principles, that 80–100 per cent of the targets be attained at level 'n', before the child can be deemed to be at level 'n'. Then, the overall result would have more meaning.

Bias and equality

The national curriculum is, of course, an entitlement curriculum. This seems the best reason for having a national curriculum and is the fiercely egalitarian philosophy underlying, for example, the French National Curriculum. Whether schools are able adequately to staff our entitlement curriculum is, of course, another matter.

John Eggleston feels that with an entitlement curriculum, and with regular formal assessment information, ethnic minority children are likely to get a fairer deal, unlike the stereotyping situation he and his colleagues observed in their case-study schools (see Chapter 5):

> If teachers and also pupils and their parents were armed with a realistic and reliable diagnosis of their capabilities then it would be possible for these disturbing and very often very destructive situations to be avoided and there is little doubt that the range of opportunities for black children would be enhanced—possibly enhanced most dramatically' (Eggleston, 1988, *op cit*).

Given the evidence on teacher stereotype and the self-fulfilling nature of teacher expectation detailed in Chapter 5, Eggleston's optimism is to be welcomed. As TGAT acknowledged, teacher assessment needs to be based on a wide range of tasks and to follow detailed guidelines, in order to reduce the effect of stereotype. However, even with this there will be scope for the teacher assessment to be affected by stereotype, for example, scores of boys and girls who perform marginally at a particular level in maths or science to be edged up or down. It is vital that the issue of stereotyping is addressed in INSET on teacher assessment.

An interesting case study of pupil allocation to maths sets in the first year of a 9–13 middle school shows quite clearly how teachers use personal knowledge and bias alongside test scores. The constructs the teachers used included: matching with older brothers and sisters; not seeming slow in working, or lazy; conforming to an ideal type ('he's definitely set 1 material'); and physical appearance ('he looks as though he should be a set 4') (Troman, 1988). This school did not contain ethnic minority children, so it is clearly a general issue rather than one related only to gender or race. As Troman points out, his work suggests that

> 'the outcomes of objective tests will do little to change teacher typifications derived from classroom interaction, and that important decisions regarding pupil allocation to different routes through schooling may be made largely on the basis of these typifications.'

The equal opportunities lesson is that you can do your best to try to make tests more gender or culture fair, but this will not make a fair society. Girls are differentially allocated to lower status maths exams; ethnic minority students are underestimated by their teachers; girls have had to do better than boys on the eleven-plus in order to get a grammar school place; girls perform better than boys in public exams yet fewer go on to higher education. And so on. Reducing bias in assessment is only part of the task.

I am labouring the point about bias and stereotype in teacher judgement because it is so important. Carefully structured teacher assessments, with a clear understanding of stereotyping and bias, must be a first step in improving teachers' judgements of children. If national assessment can deliver this we shall have much to be grateful for.

Formative and summative tensions

It is important to remember that national assessment has two distinct parts: there is the detailed, *formative* assessment information that makes up the child's profile of attainment and will be used as the basis of communication about individual children to parents and other teachers. This part of national assessment, the descriptive part, could be extremely valuable for all concerned. It is the *summative*, aggregated assessment information, that has to be published, which is of less use in professional terms. The aggregated summative information is there for accountability and political purposes: it is there to evaluate and monitor schools rather than to help directly in the education of individual children.

There is a debate about the extent to which any assessment system can serve both formative and summative functions without the summative overwhelming the formative. The received wisdom at the moment amongst most educationalists is that the two cannot co-exist. Whether the dichotomy is put in terms of: educational/ selective; diagnostic/grading; or formative/summative, the summative role will always ultimately overwhelm the formative. However, given the novel structure of national assessment, it may be that the 'superiority of the summative over the formative' is not inevitable. Nevertheless, the decision that SAT results will be 'preferred' to teacher assessment, for reporting purposes rather than an overall moderated result being used, does not bode well in this regard.

The teachers' role

The TGAT model relied on teacher assessment, with moderation between this and the SAT score where there was any discrepancy, although the small print always made it clear that in the event of any *ultimate* disagreement, the SAT score was to dominate. We have now lost much (and ultimately perhaps all) of the moderation. Teachers will assess the children on all the attainment targets and this will be followed by the formal SAT assessment, which will supersede the teacher assessment where an attainment target is assessed by both. This is a disappointment, but there is scope for teachers to have a professional role in national assessment, as long as teachers' own assessments form the basis of assessment *during* the key stages i.e. leading up to reporting.

Professional assessment focuses on individual progress and performance and at its best involves a partnership between teacher and student and an absence of competition (Gipps and Goldstein, 1989). The main beneficiary of assessment must be the individual child, and therefore the main purposes must be diagnosis and motivation. The latter has been important in the development of many new approaches to assessment: graded tests, records of achievement, and aspects of GCSE.

Motivation, however, is little addressed in TGAT, although as already discussed, the underlying model (not explicitly acknowledged in the report) is one of graded assessment.

One lesson of the records of achievement developments (Broadfoot *et al*, 1988) has been that where teachers and students discuss progress and assessments in a fair and open way, then significant changes can take place in student motivation, confidence and attitude to learning. It is vital, therefore, that there is room for this process within the national assessment arrangements.

One way to enhance teachers' professional role in national assessment would be to use the SATs as a testing *and* learning device. By observing children carrying out assessment tasks (as the APU has done with diagnostic interviews), by prompting where the child gets stuck or goes wrong, teachers really can begin to assess what children know, understand and can do.

But this is not assessment as traditionally conceived. From a traditional perspective, 'helping' a student during assessment is associated with 'cheating'. A more dynamic view involves teachers as active participants in a process that does not separate assessment from the process of learning. This will clearly rely more heavily on teacher judgement and hence on adequate training.

This kind of assessment has typically been the province of the educational psychologist (or advisory teacher) in the past. But these skills should become a part of every teacher's repertoire. They are not so complex that they need to be restricted to one professional group and the SAT may well be the peg upon which to hang this new hat.

Teachers should become competent assessors themselves and have an enhanced role within the national assessment framework. Assessment is, after all, a tool for teachers, to be used for the benefit of children. The alternative to this view is to see teachers as technicians, operating an imposed, highly structured and standardised assessment which is all the more straitening because of its pervasiveness. The former will involve more work and training, but has more to offer both teachers and children.

Competition

The rhetoric of the Education Reform Act and national assessment demands an injection of competition into the education system. Torsten Husen, who has spent many years studying assessment programmes in various countries, warns about the dangers of a highly competitive assessment system within a 'meritocratic' society which pays lip service to equality of opportunity: 'A formally equal treatment in a competitive milieu does not lead to greater equality of outcomes' (Husen, 1983). Rather he suggests it is likely to produce a new underclass: those who, by virtue of their background or ability, do not succeed in the education system, do not win in the academic competition and are thus powerless in our highly technological society. The 'old' underclass, he argues, was made up of those who had no access to advanced education, while the 'new' underclass consists of those who, in theory, have equal access, but from the beginning tend to be school failures. They tend to come from unprivileged homes (though not necessarily in material terms) and their parents often have lower levels of education; very early on in their school careers these children give up competing for success; they are highly 'over-represented among truants, non-readers, vandals' and in the long run, the jobless. These children have been encouraged by the promise of equality, but defeated by the workings of a meritocratic society. The more competitive and differentiated our education system is, the more noticeable the failures, the underclass, will be.

In Chapter 6 we looked at some of the implications of national curriculum assessment for primary schools. One of the issues addressed was grouping and the NCC suggestion that grouping by age may no longer be the most appropriate. Most observers are agreed that with national assessment there will be an increase in differentiation among children. Indeed this is one of the things that the TGAT model was designed to encourage. It is unlikely that we will return to streaming, since that entails keeping children of the same age together, but what is likely to happen is that strict age grouping will start to go and children will be grouped by the level of attainment they have reached. Whatever it is called, it will be ability grouping rather than mixed- ability grouping.

What might be the implications of this sort of grouping? We are talking about something far more formalised and public than the informal grouping by attainment within class which many of our primary and lower secondary teachers do now. Joan Barker Lunn's classic study of *Streaming in the Primary School* which was carried out in the 1960s has some pointers. She found that the children's *academic* performance was, in the main, unaffected by whether they were in streamed or unstreamed schools, although the (few) children who were promoted or demoted in streamed schools were most certainly affected—those promoted 'taking off' and those demoted, deteriorating. 'The most striking finding was that the emotional and social development of children of average and below average ability was strongly affected by streaming or non-streaming and by teachers' attitudes'. Specifically these childrens' attitude to the class they were in, their perceived notion of other people's view of the class they were in, and their motivation to do well in school, were all more positive in unstreamed schools. By contrast, above-average children had favourable attitudes wherever they were (Barker Lunn, 1970).

Certainly we will need to be concerned about the self-esteem and motivation of less able children once the new differentiated system comes into effect. Although we are not to have *redoublement*, spending two or three years in the Level Two class and being grouped with younger children may amount to the same thing. The added complication here as far as grouping is concerned is that children are unlikely to be at the same level across a range of attainment targets or subjects.

Many schools group children by ability from 12 or 13 on, and many would accept that this is necessary. What is less acceptable, in my view, is starting this process with children as young as seven. However, there is little doubt that one way of reducing the product of the $33 \times 30 \times 3 \times 3$ sum would be to reduce the number of levels in a class. Grouping by level would achieve this. Not all primary schools are big enough to re-group like this and indeed many may not want to, but it is being encouraged and it may have instructional benefits and I use the word *instructional*, rather than educational, advisedly.

Positive outcomes

One instructional benefit which this sort of careful grouping of children will offer, whether it is within classes or across classes, is better match. By reducing the range of ability within a teaching group, the match between level of instruction and level of attainment can be increased; if match is good, learning is more likely to occur, as again we discussed in Chapter 6. It is extremely difficult to get the match right for 25–30 children within mixed ability classes in an unstructured system. The use of structured programmes of study, together with hierarchically ordered statements of attainment, their regular assessment, and a more differentiated system where children are grouped and taught by level of attainment rather than age, promise together to make better match a more realistic target for teachers.

Something else which is likely to improve under the national curriculum and assessment arrangements, with the structured system of levels of attainment, is continuity and progression. Planning and coverage from one year to the next and from one stage of schooling to the next, and the child's steady progress through these years and stages, is clearly going to be much facilitated. This, indeed, was one of the principal benefits envisaged by the architects of the national curriculum.

The amount and type of information which parents will receive about their children's achievements, progress and future work will help enormously in the dialogue between parents and schools. Hopefully, teachers will welcome this aspect of national curriculum and assessment and go forward positively in opening up their work to parents; it has been a failure of post-Plowden primary education to explain to parents, despite parental involvement in the early stages of schooling, what their children are doing and why.

However, the problem in explaining national assessment results to individual parents lies in their very complexity and the sheer number of assessments for each child. Teachers are going to have to do a major job in summarising and simplifying the details. This is not meant as a patronising comment on parents; any one who has tried to get to grips with national assessment knows how complex it is and that a 15 minute slot at parents evening will not be enough to explain it in detail.

Raising standards

The DES has described the introduction of the national curriculum and assessment as a proven and acceptable way of raising standards (DES, 1987a). But there is little *evidence* that the introduction of mandated testing raises 'standards' short of teaching to the test and teaching to the test is usually narrowing. However, what we have here is the introduction of mandated testing linked to specific curriculum objectives (the statements of attainment) and a high significance placed on the results.

This is what the Americans call Measurement Driven Instruction or MDI involving:

> '. . . the use of high-stakes achievement tests to direct the instructional process. The logic of MDI is that when an important consequence or a high stake, such as obtaining a high school diploma or a teaching

certificate, is tied to test performance, the content reflected in the test will be incorporated into instruction. The consequence associated with test performance will force an instructional response and the content of the test will "drive" instruction. The higher the stakes, the greater the impact on instruction.' (Airasian, 1988)

We have already dealt with high-stakes testing (in Chapter 1) and the likely significance of national assessment; other boundary conditions for MDI are equally relevant:

'First, criterion-referenced tests must be used to clarify the skills and knowledge that will be measured and to provide the "instructional targets" for teachers. Second, nontrivial knowledge and skills, including higher level behaviours, must be measured. Third, a manageable number of skills or objectives should be measured, with the skills or objectives being sufficiently general to subsume lower level enabling skills and knowledge. Fourth, instructional clarity must be attained, so that teachers can use the targeted objectives as a basis for planning instruction. Fifth, instructional support, useful instructional materials, and suggestions for how skills can be taught must be part of the program.' (Airasian, 1988, *op cit*)

All but the last of these are key features of national assessment, although we are likely to have an unmanageable number of skills and objectives at first. But, particularly interestingly, Airasian points out that the greatest impact on instruction will occur when high standards *and* high stakes are present and national curriculum assessment is not a minimum competency, but almost a maximum competency, assessment. Various European external examinations, such as the English O- and A-level exams, are given by Airasian as examples of high-stakes, high-standards testing programmes; stakes are high and standards are more than minimal. It is well documented that such exams are very influential in driving the school curriculum.

There can be little doubt that, given the structure and significance of national curriculum assessment, standards of performance on the assessments will rise as teachers become familiar with the curriculum and assessment arrangements and gear their teaching towards them. And in this completely novel system, with ultimately a wide range of subjects being tested, if the curriculum is good and wide and if the assessments are educationally valid and enabling, we may have to change conventional notions about teaching to the test; it may not be such a cause for concern as it is with limited testing of a narrow range of subjects. Unfortunately, however, it is the very scope of the assessment system that is likely to make it unworkable.

But again, we must consider these developments in context.

National assessment, within the wider framework of the Education Reform Act, encourages competition among schools. There is likely to be more selectivity at school level, while the assessments will lead to more differentiation within schools. The point about a competition is that the best will win; the point about differentiation is that the more able should not be held back. All will do better but the most able will still win the competition, and the competition will start much younger. So, average standards *can* be expected to rise. But at what cost, it must be asked, within this competitive milieu, to the less able student, the linguistic minority student, the student with special needs, the disadvantaged? It will be five or even ten years' time before we can answer that question.

I shall finish, as this book began, with history. Here is an extract from a book by Edmond Holmes, Chief Inspector for Elementary Schools, who published in 1911 a reflection on education over the previous 50 years, including Payment by Results (Holmes, 1911, pp. 103–109). This system, which stifled elementary education and profoundly affected the role of HMI (turning them from advisers to examiners) actually collapsed under its own administrative weight. The differences between Payment by Results and national assessment, between the Revised Code and the Education Reform Act are obvious. But some similarities are striking and much of what he writes encapsulates the fears of teachers now. Perhaps this time we could learn the lesson of history.

'The State, in prescribing a syllabus which was to be followed, in all the subjects of instruction, by all the schools in the country, without regard to local or personal considerations, was guilty of one capital offence. It did all his thinking for the teacher. It told him in precise detail what he was to do each year in each "Standard", how he was to handle each subject, and how far he was to go in it; what width of ground he was to cover; what amount of knowledge, what degree of accuracy was required for a "pass". In other words it provided him with his ideals, his general conceptions, his more immediate aims, his schemes of work; and if it did not control his methods in all their details, it gave him (by implication) hints and suggestions with regard to these on which he was not slow to act; for it told them that the work done in each class and each subject would be tested at the end of each year by a careful examination of each individual child; and it was inevitable that in his endeavour to adapt his teaching to the type of question which his experience of the yearly examination led him to expect, he should gradually deliver himself, mind and soul, into the hands of the officials of the Department—the officials at Whitehall who framed the yearly syllabus, and the officials in the various districts who examined on it.

What the Department did to the teacher, it compelled him to do to the child. The teacher who is the slave of another's will cannot carry out his instructions except by making his pupils the slaves of his own will. The teacher who has been deprived by his superiors of freedom, initiative, and responsibility, cannot carry out his instructions except by depriving his pupils of the same vital qualities' . . .

. . . 'To be in bondage to a syllabus is a misfortune for a teacher, and a misfortune for the school that he teaches. To be in bondage to a syllabus which is binding on all schools alike, is a graver misfortune. To be in bondage to a bad syllabus which is binding on all schools alike, is of all misfortunes the gravest.

Of the evils that are inherent in the examination system as such – of its tendency to arrest growth, to deaden life, to paralyse the higher faculties, to externalise what is inward, to materialise what is spiritual, to involve education in an atmosphere of unreality and self-deception – I have already spoken at some length. In the days of payment by results various circumstances conspired to raise those evil tendencies to the highest imaginable "power". When inspectors ceased to examine (in the stricter sense of the word) they realised what infinite mischief the yearly examination had done.' . . .

. . . 'Not a thought was given, except in a small minority of the schools, to the real training of the child, to the fostering of his mental (and other) growth. To get him through the yearly examination by hook or by crook was the one concern of the teacher. As profound distrust of the teacher was the basis of the policy of the Department, so profound distrust of the child was the basis of the policy of the teacher. To leave the child to find out anything for himself, to work out anything for himself, would have been regarded as a proof of incapacity, not to say insanity, on the part of the teacher, and would have led to results which, from the 'percentage' point of view, would probably have been disastrous.'

Few people want to go back to those days, but we need to make sure that we do not, for the potential is there for an assessment system which is unwieldy, judgemental, summative, fragmenting, high stakes and instruction-driving. What we need instead is a system in which the educational and formative purposes of assessment are paramount, and in which teachers have a key professional role.

Bibliography

Airasian, P. (1988) 'Measurement Driven Instruction: A Closer Look', *Educational Measurement: Issues and Practice*, Winter 1988.

APU (1986) *A Review of Monitoring in Maths 1978–82*, DES.

APU (1988) *Attitudes and Gender Differences. Mathematics at Age 11 and 15* Windsor: NFER/Nelson.

Balogh, J. (1982) *Profile Reports for School Leavers*, York: Longmans.

Barker Lunn, J. (1970) *Streaming in the Primary School*, Windsor: NFER.

Becher, T., Eraut, M., Barton, J., Canning, T. and Knight, J. (1980) *Accountability in the Middle Years of Schooling*, Part 1 Report to SSRC.

Bennett, N., Desforges, C., Cockburn, A. and Wilkinson, B. (1984) *The Quality of Pupil Learning Experiences*, London: Lawrence Erlbaum Associates.

Bogdanor, V. (1979) *Standards in Schools*, National Council for Educational Standards.

Bourdieu, P. and Passeron, J. C. (1976) *Reproduction in Education Society and Culture*, London: Sage Publications.

Burt, C. (1921) *Mental and Scholastic Tests*, London: King and Son.

Burt, C. (1937) *The Backward Child*, (1961 Edition) University of London Press Ltd.

Broadfoot, P. (1979) *Assessment, Schools and Society*, London: Methuen.

Broadfoot, P. (1986) *Profiles and Records of Achievement: A Review of Issues and Practice*, London: Holt, Reinhardt and Winston.

Broadfoot, P. and Osborn, M. (1987) 'French Lessons', *The Times Educational Supplement*, 3 July.

Broadfoot, P., James, M., McMeeking, S., Nuttall, D. and Stierer, B. (1988) *Records of Achievement*, Report of the National Evaluation of Pilot Schemes. London: HMSO.

Brown, M. (1983) 'Graded tests in mathematics: the implications of various models for the mathematics curriculum', paper presented at BERA conference, London: September 1983.

Brown, M. (1988) Issues in 'Formulating and organising Attainment

Targets in Relation to their Assessment' in *National Assessment and Testing: A Research Response* Ed. H. Torrance BERA.

Brown, M. (1989) 'Graded Assessment and Learning Hierarchies in Mathematics – an alternative view'. *British Education Research Journal*, 15, 2.

Cambridge Institute of Education (1985) *'New perspectives on the mathematics curriculum: an independent appraisal of the outcomes of APU mathematics testing 1978–82'*, London: HMSO.

Chisholm, L. (1987), *'Vorsprung ex machina?* Aspects of curriculum and assessment in cultural comparison', *Journal of Education Policy*, 2, 2, pp. 149–59.

Christie, T. and Forrest, G. M. (1980) *Standards at GCE A-level: 1963 and 1973*, London: Macmillan Educational.

Christie, T. and Forrest, G. M. (1981) *Defining Public Examination Standards*, London: Macmillan Educational.

Clift, P., Weiner, G. and Wilson, E. (1981) *Record Keeping in the Primary School*, Basingstoke Schools Council: Macmillan.

Coleman, J. S., Campbell, E., Hobson, C., McPartland, J., Mood, A., Weinfeld, F. and York, R. (1966) *Equality of Educational Opportunity*, Washington National Centre for Educational Statistics.

Corbett, H. D. and Wilson, B. (1988) 'Raising the stakes in statewide mandatory minimum competency testing', in *1988 Year Book of the Politics of Education Association, Journal of Education Policy*, Vol. 3 No. 5.

Cresswell, M. (1989) 'Two Issues in GCSE Maths: coursework and differentiated papers', paper delivered to HMI conference 'GCSE Maths', Birmingham: 20–22 March 1989.

Davie, R., Butler, N. R. and Goldstein, H. (1972) *From Birth to Seven*, London: Longman.

Deale, R. N. (1975) *Assessment and Testing in the Secondary School*, London: Evans/Methuen Educational.

DES (1967) *Children and their Primary Schools*, The Plowden Report, London: HMSO.

DES (1975) *A Language for Life* (Bullock Report), London: HMSO.

DES (1978a) *School Examinations: report of the Steering Committee established to reconsider proposals for replacing the GCE O level and CSE examinations* (Waddell Report) Part 1 HMSO Cmnd. 7281.

DES (1978b) *Secondary School Examinations: a single system at 16+* (White Paper) HMSO Cmnd. 7368.

DES (1982) *Mathematics Counts: Report of the committee of inquiry into the teaching of mathematics in schools*, London: HMSO.

DES (1984) *Records of Achievement: a statement of policy*, London: HMSO.

DES (1985) *GCSE: National Criteria*, London: HMSO.

DES (1986) *English School Leavers: 1983–4*, DES Statistical Bulletin 4/86, London: HMSO.

DES (1987a) *The National Curriculum 5–16: A Consultation Document*, DES/Welsh Office.

DES (1987b) *Improving the Basis For Awarding GCSE Grades*, unpublished paper, September 1987 (made available to TGAT).

DES (1988a) *National Curriculum: Task Group on Assessment and Testing: A Report*, DES/Welsh Office.

DES (1988b) Draft Circular – *The Education Reform Act: Information Requirements Relating to the School Curriculum and Assessment*, September 1988, DES/Welsh Office.

DES (1989a) *The National Curriculum: from policy to practice*, DES/Welsh Office.

DES (1989b) *English School Leavers: 1986–7*, DES Statistical Bulletin, London: HMSO.

DES (1989c) 'Kenneth Baker welcomes successful introduction of GCSE', July 21, Press Notice 235/89.

Douglas, J. W. B., Ross, J. M. and Simpson, H. (1968) *All Our Future*, Peter Davies.

Eggleston, J. (1984) 'School Examinations—Some Sociological Issues', in Broadfoot, P. (Ed) *Selection, Certification and Control*, Lewes: Falmer Press.

Eggleston, J. (1988) 'The New Education Bill and Assessment—some implications for black children', *Multicultural Teaching*, 6, 2, Spring.

Eggleston, J., Dunn, D., Anjali, M. and Wright, C. (1986) *Education for Some*, Stoke on Trent: Trentham Books.

Essen, J. and Ghodsian, M. (1979) 'The children of immigrants: school performance', *New Community*, 1, 3.

Faggen, J. (1987) 'Golden Rule Revisited: Introduction', *Educational Measurement: Issues and Practice*, 6, 2, Summer.

Fogelman, K., Goldstein, H., Essen, J. and Ghodsian, M. (1978) 'Patterns of Attainment', *Educational Studies*, 4, pp. 121–130.

Gipps, C. (1986) 'The GCSE: some background', in *The GCSE: an uncommon Exam*, Bedford Way Papers, No. 29 C. Gipps (Ed).

Gipps, C. (1987a) 'The APU: from Trojan Horse to Angel of Light', *Curriculum*, 8, 1.

Gipps, C. (1987b) Differentiation in GCSE, *Forum*, 29, 3.

Gipps, C. (1988a) 'The TGAT Report: Trick or Treat?', *Forum*, 31, 1.

Gipps, C. (1988b) *The Experience of Differentiation in GCSE*, unpublished paper.

Gipps, C. and Goldstein, H. (1983) *Monitoring Children: an evaluation of the Assessment of Performance Unit*, London: Heinemann Educational Books.

Gipps, C. and Goldstein, H. (1989) 'A Curriculum for Teacher Assessment', *Journal of Curriculum Studies*, 21, 6.

Gipps, C., Gross, H. and Goldstein, H. (1987) *Warnock's Eighteen Percent: Children with special needs in primary schools*, Lewes: Falmer Press.

Gipps, C., Steadman, S., Blackstone, T. and Stierer, B. (1983) *Testing Children: Standardised Testing in Schools and LEAs*, London: Heinemann Educational Books.

Gipps, C. and Wood, R. (1981) 'The Testing of Reading in LEAs: the Bullock Report Seven Years On', *Educational Studies*, 7, 2.

Goldstein, H. (1983) 'Measuring changes in educational attainment over time: problems and possibilities', *Journal of Educational Measurement*, 20, 4, Winter.

Goldstein, H. (1986) 'Gender Bias and Test Norms in Educational Selection', *Research Intelligence*, (BERA Newsletter) May 1986.

Goldstein, H. (1987) *Multilevel Models in Educational and Social Research*, London: Charles Griffin and Co.

Goldstein, H. (1988) *National Testing and Equal Opportunities*, Appendix to TGAT Report, DES.

Goldstein, H. and Cuttance, P. (1988) 'National Assessment and School Comparisons', *Journal of Education Policy*, Vol. 3, No. 2.

Goldstein, H. and Woodhouse, G. (1988) *Educational Performance Indicators and LEA League Tables*, London: ULIE.

Good, F. and Cresswell, M. (1988) *Grading the GCSE*, London: SEC.

Guskey, T. R. and Kifer, E. W. (1989) *Ranking School Districts on the basis of Statewide Test Results: Is it meaningful or misleading?*. Paper presented at AERA Conference San Francisco, March 1989.

Hargreaves, D. H. (1982) *The Challenge for the Comprehensive School*, London: Routledge and Kegan Paul.

Hargreaves, A. (1986) Record Breakers? in *Profiles and Records of Achievement*, Ed. P. Broadfoot, London: Holt, Reinhart and Winston.

Hargreaves, A. (1988) 'The Crisis of Motivation and Assessment' in Hargreaves, A. and Reynolds, D. *Education Policies: Controversies and Critiques*, Lewes: Falmer Press.

Harlen, W. (1982) 'The Role of Assessment in Matching', *Primary Education Review*, 13, Spring.

Harrison, A. (1982) *A Review of Graded Tests*, London: Methuen/ Schools Council Exam Bulletin 41.

Hart, K., Johnson, D. C., Brown, M., Dickson, L. and Clarkson, R. (1989) *Children's Mathematical Frameworks: 8–13*, Windsor: NFER-Nelson.

Hannon, P. and McNally, J. (1986) 'Children's Understanding and Cultural Factors in Reading Test Performance', *Educational Review*, 38, 3.

HMI (1978) *Primary Education in England*, A survey by HMI, London: HMSO.

HMI (1979) *Aspects of Secondary Education in England*, A survey by HMI, London: HMSO.

HMI (1983) *Records of Achievement at 16: some examples of current practice*, London: HMSO.

HMI (1986) *Education in the Federal Republic of Germany: aspects of curriculum and assessment*, London: HMSO.

HMI (1988) *The Introduction of the GCSE in schools 1986–88*, London: HMSO.

Holmes, E. (1911) *What Is and What Might Be*, London: Constable and Co. Ltd.

House, E. (1978) 'An American view of British Accountability', in Becher, T. and Maclure, S. (Eds) *Accountability in Education*, Windsor: NFER.

Husen, T. (1983) 'Are standards in US schools really lagging behind those in other countries?', *Phi Delta Kappan*, March 1983.

ILEA (1983) *Race, Sex and Class 1. Achievement in Schools*, London: ILEA.

ILEA (1984) *Improving Secondary Schools* (The Hargreaves Report) London: ILEA.

ILEA (1987) *Ethnic Background and Examination Results 1985 and 1986* Report No. RS 1120/87 ILEA Research and Statistics Branch.

JCTP (1988) *Code of Fair Testing Practices in Education*, Joint Committee on Testing Practices APA Washington D.C. USA.

Kellaghan, T., Madaus, G. and Airasian, P. (1982) *The Effects of Standardised Testing*, Boston: Kluwer Nijhoff Publishing.

Kent Mathematics Project (1978) *KMP Teachers Guide Levels 1–4*, London: Ward Lock Educational.

Kingdon, M. and Stobart, G. (1987) *The Draft Grade Criteria: A Review of LEAG Research*, LEAG Discussion Paper.

Kingdon, M. and Stobart, G. (1988) *GCSE Examined*, Lewes: Falmer Press.

Laycock, E. (1989) 'Testing Reading . . . an Investigation', in *Testing Reading*, London: CLPE, ILEA.

Lawton, D. (1984) *'The Tightening Grip: the growth of central control of the school curriculum'*, Bedford Way, Paper No. 21 ULIE.

Lawton, D. (1987) 'The role of legislation in educational standards', *NUT Education Review*, 1, 1.

Little, A. (1975) 'Performance of Children from Ethnic Minority Backgrounds in Primary Schools', *Oxford Review of Education*, 1, 2.

Mabey, C. (1981) 'Black British Literacy: a study of reading attainment of London black children from 8 to 15 years', *Educational Research*, 23, 2.

MacDonald, B. (1978) 'Accountability, standards and the process of schooling', in Becher, T. and Maclure, S. (Eds) 1978, *Accountability in Education*, Windsor: NFER.

McEwan, A., Canadan, S. and Salters, J. (1988) *Graded Objectives in French: Attitudes in Northern Ireland Schools*, Queen's University: School of Education.

Mackintosh, N. J. and Mascie-Taylor, C. (1985) 'The IQ Question' *Annex D The Swann Report, Education for All*, London: HMSO.

MacIntyre, A. (1989) 'Evaluating Schools', M. Preedy (Ed) *Approaches to Curriculum Management*, Open University Press.

McNaughton, T. (1989) 'Exam Questions: A consideration of consequences of reforms to examining and assessment in Great Britain and New Zealand', BCIES Conference 1988 Proceedings, in *Changing Educational Assessment: International Perspectives and Trends*, Eds R. Murphy, H. Torrance and P. Broadfoot (at press) London: Routledge.

Madaus, G. (1988) 'The influence of testing on the curriculum', in L. Tanner (Ed) *Critical Issues in Curriculum*, 87th Year Book of NSSE, Part 1, University of Chicago Press.

Mortimore, P. (1983) 'Graded Tests: a challenge or a problem?', *Paper presented to the British Educational Research Association Annual Conference*, London: 1983.

Mortimore, J. and Mortimore, P. (1984) *Secondary School Examinations*, ULIE: Bedford Way Paper No. 18.

Mortimore, P., Sammons, P., Stoll, L., Lewis, D. and Ecob, R. (1988) *School Matters: the junior years*, Hove: Lawrence Erlbaum Associates.

Murphy, P. (1989) 'Assessment and Gender', *NUT Education Review*, 3, 2.

Murphy, R. J. (1982) Sex Differences in Objective Test Performance, *British Journal Educational Psychology*, 52, 213–219.

Murphy, R. J. (1986a) 'A Revolution in Educational Assessment?', *Forum*, 28, 2.

Murphy, R. (1986b) 'The Emperor Has No Clothes: grade criteria and the GCSE', in *The GCSE: An uncommon exam* (Ed) C. Gipps, ULIE: Bedford Way paper No. 29.

Murphy, R. J. (1987) 'Pupil Assessment in Primary Schools', *Forum*, 30, 1.

National Curriculum Council (1989) *Implementing the National Curriculum in Primary Schools*, Circular No. 3 NCC.

Noss, R., Goldstein, H. and Hoyles, C. (1989) 'Graded Assessment and Learning Hierarchies in Mathematics', *BERJ*, 15, 2.

Nuttall, D. (1987) 'Testing, Testing, Testing . . .' *NUT Education Review*, 1, 2.

Nuttall, D. (1988) 'National Assessment: Complacency or Misinterpretation?', Public Lecture given on 2nd March 1988 at ULIE published in D. Lawton (Ed) *The Education Reform Act: Choice and Control*, (1989) London: Hodder and Stoughton.

Nuttall, D. (1989) 'National Assessment—Will Reality Match Aspirations?', Paper delivered to the conference *'Testing Times'*, Macmillan Education, 8 April, 1989.

Nuttall, D. and Goldstein, H. (1984) 'Profiles and Graded Tests: the technical issues', in Mortimore, J. (Ed) *Profiles in Action*, London: Further Education Unit.

Nuttall, D., Goldstein, H., Prosser, R. and Rasbash, H. (1989) 'Differential School Effectiveness', *International Journal of Educational Research* (at press).

Orr, R. and Nuttall, D. (1983) *Determining Standards in the Proposed System of Examining at 16 plus*, Comparability in Examinations, Occasional Paper 2, London: Schools Council.

Pennycuick, D. and Murphy, R. (1986) 'The impact of the Graded Test Movement on Classroom Teaching and Learning', *Studies in Educational Evaluation*, 12, 1986.

Pennycuick, D. and Murphy, R. (1988) *The Impact of Graded Tests*, Lewes: Falmer Press.

Plewis, I. *et al* (1981) *Publishing School Examination results – A Discussion*, Bedford Way Paper 5.

Raban, B. (1983) *Guides to Assessment in Education: Reading*, London: Macmillan Education.

Rampton, (1981) *West Indian Children in our Schools*, CMND 8273 London: HMSO.

Resnick, D. P. (1980) 'Educational policy and the applied historian: testing, competency and standards', *Journal of Social History*, June 1980.

Richmond, J. (1984) 'Staging English', *The English Magazine*, Summer 1984.

Rosen, H. (1982) *The Language Monitors*, Bedford Way Paper No. 11, ULIE.

Rutter, M., Yule, W. and Berger, M. (1974) 'The Children of West Indian Migrants', *New Society*, 14 March.

Rutter, M., Maughan, B., Mortimore, P. and Ouston, J. (1979)

Fifteen Thousand Hours, London: Open Books.

Salmon-Cox, L. (1981) 'Teachers and Standardised Achievement Tests: what's really happening?', *Phi Delta Kappan*, May.

School's Council (1971) *A Common System of Examining at 16 Plus*, Schools Bulletin 23, Evans/Methuen.

Scott, D. (1989) 'HMI reporting of the GSCE', *Journal of Education Policy*, 4, 3.

SEC (1984) *The Development of Grade-Related Criteria for the GCSE. A briefing paper for working parties*, London: SEC.

SEC (1985) *Differentiated Assessment in GCSE*, Working Paper One, London: SEC.

SEAC (1989) *Progress Report on the GCSE*, July 1989.

Simons, H. (1988) *Evaluating Schools in a Democracy*, Lewes: Falmer Press.

Skilbeck, M. (1977) 'The flight from education', *Education News*, Vol. 16, No. 3.

Smith, D. and Tomlinson, S. (1989) *The School Effect*, London Policy Studies Institute.

Smith, P. and Whetton, C. (1988) 'Bias Reduction in Test Development', *The Psychologist*, July 1988.

Statistical Information Service (1988) *Performance Indicators for Schools—a Consultation Document*, The Chartered Institute of Public Finance and Accountancy.

Stibbs, A. (1981) *Assessing Children's Language*, London: Ward Lock/NATE.

Stierer, B. (1989) 'Reading Tests', in *Testing Reading*, London: CLPE, ILEA.

Stobart, G. (1987) *Differentiation: A Review of LEAG Research*, Unpublished Paper, ULSEB.

Sutherland, G. (1984) *Ability, Merit and Measurement: Mental testing and English education, 1880–1940*, Oxford University Press.

Sutherland, G. (1987) *Evidence to TGAT*, unpublished.

Swann, M. (1985) *Education for All*, Cmnd 9453, London: HMSO.

Taylor, J. and Wallace, G. (1988) 'GCSE: Some Dilemmas in Implementing the Criteria for Continuous Assessment in English', Paper given to BERA Conference 1988, published in *British Journal of Sociology of Education*, 11, 2, 1990.

Thom, D. (1986) 'The 1944 Education Act: the "art of the possible"' in *War and Social Change: British Society in the Second World War* (Ed) Hal Smith, Manchester University Press.

Thomas, N. (1982) 'Testing and Assessing', *Primary Education Review*, No. 13.

Thomson, G. O. B. and Sharp, S. (1988) 'History of Mental Testing', in J. Keeves (Ed) *Educational Research Methodology* and Measurement: An International Handbook, Oxford: Pergamon.

Thornton, G. (1986) APU Language Testing 1979–1983: an independent appraisal of the findings, London: HMSO.

Tizard, B., Blatchford, P., Burke, J., Farquar, C. and Plewis, I. (1988) Young Children at School in the Inner City, Hove: Lawrence Erlbaum Associates.

Townsend, H. and Brittan, E. (1972) Organisation in Multi-racial Schools, Windsor: NFER.

Troman, G. (1988) 'Getting it Right: selection and setting in a 9–13 middle school', British Journal of Sociology of Education, 9, 4.

Vincent, D. (1985) Reading Tests in the Classroom: an introduction, Windsor: NFER/Nelson.

Walden, R. and Walkerdine, V. (1985) Girls and Mathematics: from primary to secondary schooling, Bedford Way Paper No. 24, ULIE.

Weiss, J. (1987) 'The Golden Rule Bias Reduction Principle: A Practical Reform', Educational Measurement: Issues and Practice, 6, 2, Summer 1987.

Wood, R. (1978) 'Sex Differences in Answers to English Language Comprehension Items', Educational Studies, 4, 157–165.

Wood, R. (1985) Testing, Unit 21 E206 Block 4 Personality, Development and Learning, Open University.

Wood, R. (1987) 'Assessment and Equal Opportunities', Text of Public lecture at ULIE (11 November 1987).

Wood, R. and Power, C. (1984) 'Have National Assessments made us any wiser about Standards?', Comparative Education, 20, 3.

Wright, C. (1987) 'Black Students – White Teachers', in Racial Inequality in Education (Ed) B. Troyna, London: Tavistock.

Yeh, J. (1978) Test Use in Schools, Centre for the Study of Evaluation, University of California, Los Angeles (unpublished).

Yule, W., Berger, M., Rutter, M. and Yule, B. (1975) 'Children of West Indian immigrants—intellectual performance and reading attainment', Journal of Child Psychology and Psychiatry, 16.

Index

Need to Know

Alzheimer's Disease

Jim McGuigan

Heinemann
LIBRARY

www.heinemann.co.uk/library

Visit our website to find out more information about **Heinemann Library** books.

To order:

☎ Phone 44 (0) 1865 888066

▤ Send a fax to 44 (0) 1865 314091

▯ Visit the Heinemann Bookshop at www.heinemann.co.uk/library to browse our catalogue and order online.

Produced by Monkey Puzzle Media Ltd
Gissing's Farm, Fressingfield, Suffolk IP21 5SH, UK

First published in Great Britain by Heinemann Library, Halley Court, Jordan Hill, Oxford OX2 8EJ, part of Harcourt Education.
Heinemann is a registered trademark of Harcourt Education Ltd.

Editorial: Katie Orchard
Design: Jane Hawkins
Picture Research: Sally Cole
Consultant: Janice Brown, Alzheimer's Society, UK
Production: Viv Hichens

Originated by Ambassador Litho Ltd
Printed and bound in Hong Kong, China by
  South China Printing Company

ISBN 0 431 18841 6 (hardback)
08 07 06 05 04
10 9 8 7 6 5 4 3 2 1

ISBN 0 431 18848 3 (paperback)
09 08 07 06 05
10 9 8 7 6 5 4 3 2 1

Some names in this text have been changed to protect the privacy of the individuals quoted

British Library Cataloguing in Publication Data
McGuigan, Jim
  Alzheimer's disease – (Need to know)
  1.Alzheimer's disease – Juvenile literature
  I.Title
  616.8'31

Acknowledgements
The publishers would like to thank the following for permission to reproduce photographs: Alamy pp. 1 (Sam Tanner/Photofusion), 12 (Plainpicture), 19 (Sam Tanner/Photofusion), 25 (Paul Baldesare/Photofusion); Corbis pp. 14 (DiMaggio/Kalish), 21 (Vo Trung [NPP] Dung/Sygma), 28 (Jose Luis Pelaez, Inc), 35 (Paul Barton), 45 (Michael Heron), 51 (Leland Bobbé); Photofusion pp. 15 (Paul Doyle), 34 (Paul Chitty), 39 (Joanne O'Brien), 41 (Joanne O'Brien); Rex Features pp. 17 (Sipa), 18 (Guzelian Photography); Sally and Richard Greenhill p. 42 (Sally Greenhill); Science Photo Library pp. 4 (Alfred Pasieka), 7 (Simon Fraser/MRC Unit, Newcastle General Hospital), 8 (Antonia Reeve), 9 (Dr W Crum, Dementia Research Group/Tim Beddow), 11 (National Library of Medicine), 20 (SIU), 37 (Chris Priest), 38–39 (Catherine Pouedras), 48 (James King-Holmes), 49; Topham Picturepoint pp. 5 (Image Works), 16 (Bob Daemmrich/Image Works), 23 (Nita Winter/Image Works), 26 (Alison Wright/Image Works), 31 (Richard Lord/Image Works), 32 (Rhoda Sidney/Image Works), 47 (Jeff Greenberg/Image Works); Wellcome Trust p. 10.

Cover photographs reproduced with permission of SPL (Will and Deni McIntyre) and SPL (Dr W. Crum, Dementia Research Group/Tim Beddow).

Every effort has been made to contact copyright holders of any material reproduced in this book. Any omissions will be rectified in subsequent printings if notice is given to the publishers.

To Maggie, for all her support during the writing of this book.

Contents

Any words appearing in the text in bold, **like this**, are explained in the Glossary.

Alzheimer's disease

Alzheimer's disease is a progressive condition that affects the brain, eventually leading to the death of brain cells. It is referred to as a progressive disease because the condition gradually becomes worse over time. Alzheimer's disease usually strikes people over the age of 65, but it can develop in people as young as 35, when it is called **early-onset disease**.

This photograph shows two brain scans. The right side is healthy tissue, and the left side shows shrinkage of brain tissue in a person with Alzheimer's disease.

Alzheimer's disease attacks nerve cells in the brain and robs people of their memories. People not only forget the names of everyday objects, they may also forget what they are. People with Alzheimer's disease may suddenly find themselves lost when walking to the shops close to their home.

Eventually the on-going damage to the brain leaves the person with Alzheimer's disease hardly able to speak. Sometimes they are unable to recognize their own husband, wife or children, and they need help to eat, wash, dress and to go the toilet. This may occur 5, 10 or even 20 years after the disease is discovered, although most people enter the final stages of the illness after about eight years.

A growing problem

As more people live into their 70s and 80s, Alzheimer's disease is going to affect many more lives. By the year 2025, it is estimated that throughout the world there will be more than 34 million people with Alzheimer's disease – incredibly, that is more than the entire population of Australia and New Zealand.

Expert care

No one can provide proper care for a person with Alzheimer's disease without the support of their family, professionals such as nurses and counsellors, and the generous help of people working for voluntary Alzheimer's organizations around the world. Many people, including family doctors, are not familiar with the symptoms of the disease and it may take years for a person to receive a correct diagnosis. Increasing knowledge and awareness of Alzheimer's disease should be the first step on the road to improving the future care of the millions of people who will be lost to this incurable illness.

❝When my mother was diagnosed with Alzheimer's disease I contacted the Alzheimer's Society (UK). They saved my life. The information and advice they gave me helped me and my family get through very difficult times.❞

(Anne Robinson, presenter of the UK TV quiz show, *The Weakest Link*)

What is Alzheimer's disease?

Alzheimer's disease is a form of **dementia**. The term 'dementia' is used to describe many different diseases of the brain that cause people to experience serious memory loss and confusion. About 1 in 20 people over the age of 65 develop dementia. More than half of these people have Alzheimer's disease, making it the most common cause of dementia. (Other forms of dementia are discussed on pages 8–9.)

A progressive disease

Alzheimer's disease is a progressive condition that affects a person's brain cells. This means that gradually the brain cells die and more parts of the brain become damaged. Over time the person's symptoms will become worse.

People experiencing the early stages of Alzheimer's disease may become forgetful or have difficulty finding the right words for everyday things. One of the first symptoms is the loss of **short-term memory** (the ability to remember recent events). For example, a 70-year-old person may remember details of their twelfth birthday party, but just a few minutes after leaving the table, they may forget that they have eaten breakfast. As the disease progresses, they may become increasingly confused. Over time the person with Alzheimer's disease will need increasing help in all activities from those who care for them.

A chemical imbalance

People with Alzheimer's disease have a shortage of important chemicals in the brain called **neurotransmitters**. Neurotransmitters are responsible for the transmission of messages within the brain. These messages control functions such as memory, ability to think clearly, speech and movement. In Alzheimer's disease, fine fibres of a **protein** called **tau** become twisted together to form **tangles** inside brain cells. These tangles build up until

A scientist examines brain tissue of a person with Alzheimer's disease under a microscope. The dark areas shown on the screen consist of thick layers (plaques) of the protein beta amyloid.

they burst the cells, causing them to die. Another protein, **beta amyloid**, builds up in layers called **plaques** in between the brain cells. These plaques are toxic (poisonous) to the brain cells and kill any lying close to them.

The gradual loss of abilities of a person with Alzheimer's disease happens as different parts of the brain become damaged – although each person will experience the disease in their own individual way. Usually, the part of the brain that is responsible for storing new memories is affected first. Later the part of the brain that is responsible for planning and carrying out tasks becomes damaged. In the final stage of the disease, the area of the brain that controls the muscles is affected, making walking and other movements difficult.

Other types of dementia

It is important for doctors to be able to tell the difference between Alzheimer's disease and other types of **dementia**. A correct diagnosis will allow the person to get the best treatment and know what to expect from their illness. The various different dementias have similar symptoms to Alzheimer's disease, but are not the same thing.

Vascular dementia

Vascular dementia is caused by too little blood reaching the brain. What usually happens is that the person suffers a small stroke. This involves the death of a small group of brain cells that are starved of blood for a minute or two. The small blood vessels, which normally carry blood to the brain cells, may be blocked for a short time by blood clots or they may have burst as a result of high blood pressure. One small stroke is often followed by another, and several of these 'mini strokes' can damage the brain, making the person forgetful and confused.

Vascular dementia can occur when high blood pressure causes a blood vessel going to the brain to burst. People who tend to have high blood pressure need to have it checked regularly.

Dementia with Lewy bodies

In this kind of dementia, tiny round blobs of **protein** called Lewy bodies build up in brain cells. They disrupt the normal functioning of the brain, leading to memory loss, an inability to think clearly, and difficulty with speaking or writing.

Frontal lobe dementia and Pick's disease

Most damage in **frontal lobe** dementia and **Pick's disease** occurs in the front part of the brain. This part of the brain is responsible for personality, behaviour and language skills. People with these forms of dementia may suddenly start to swear more or behave inappropriately. They may also find it difficult to make plans.

Alchohol-related dementia

People who drink too much alcohol over a long period of time may cause damage to the part of the brain that controls **short-term memory**. People with this condition may also have difficulty acquiring new information or skills.

This scan shows a section of the brain of a person who has dementia with Lewy bodies. The brain (shown in orange) has atrophied (shrunk), leaving holes (shown in blue) at the bottom left and right, and large, fluid-filled areas in the centre.

Creutzfeldt-Jacob disease (CJD)

Creutzfeldt-Jacob disease (CJD) results from **prions** (infectious protein particles) attacking the nervous system and the brain, causing dementia. CJD progresses rapidly and is often fatal within one year. In 1994 a special form of CJD, called Variant CJD, was identified. It affected people of all ages and is believed to have been caused by eating meat from cows suffering from a similar disease called bovine spongiform encephalopathy (BSE) – also known as 'mad cow disease'.

History of Alzheimer's disease

Symptoms of memory loss and confusion, similar to those of Alzheimer's disease, have been seen written in ancient Egyptian, Greek and Roman texts. Descriptions of **dementia**-like illnesses have also been recorded throughout the centuries. But it was not until the early 20th century that Alzheimer's disease was recognized as a condition in its own right.

Middle Ages

In Europe in the Middle Ages, many scholars thought that all mental illnesses, including what we now call Alzheimer's disease, were caused by evil spirits entering a person and taking control of their body and mind. Treatments could be very harsh, and many people were chained up and beaten in an attempt to drive away the evil spirits.

Asylums

In the 18th century a more rigorous form of scientific and medical thinking began to spread throughout the world. It became known as the '**Age of Enlightenment**'. People were now less interested in following traditional beliefs; they wanted to gain greater knowledge and understanding (enlightenment) by using logic and reason. People with dementia were often sent to **asylums** (institutions that were specially built to hold mentally ill people). Asylums were unpleasant places, over-crowded with people who were often chained up and badly cared for.

It was not until about the mid-1850s that an increased understanding of mental illness brought significant changes in the whole approach to

This hospital in Paris, in 1857, was one of the first for patients with mental illnesses, including dementia.

treatment. Most people were then taken out of asylums and looked after in hospitals. Doctors began actively studying mental illnesses in an attempt to find out what caused them.

Recent discoveries

In 1906 a German **neurologist**, Dr Alois Alzheimer, found peculiar changes in the brain tissue of a woman who had died from what was thought to be an unusual mental illness. The woman, called Auguste, suffered from **depression**, **hallucinations** and dementia and died aged only 55. Experts soon realized the importance of the discovery and named the condition Alzheimer's disease. Alzheimer's disease was thought to be a rare illness until the 1970s, when experts realized that most people who had senile (old age) dementia and pre-senile (young age) dementia actually had Alzheimer's disease.

The first drug treatments for Alzheimer's disease were developed during the 1990s. These treatments were unable to cure the disease but could at least slow down the progression of symptoms for a little while.

Dr Alois Alzheimer, who first identified the disease.

A family connection?

Alzheimer's disease does sometimes run in families. But this is very rare, and explains only part of the picture. In most cases the disease seems to strike people 'out of the blue'. More research is needed to explain why.

Genes and early-onset disease

Some people develop Alzheimer's disease at the age of 35–65. This is called **early-onset disease**. Although rare, about 50 per cent of people with

early-onset disease have inherited the condition from their parents through a defective (faulty) **gene**.

Genes are like tiny parcels of information that determine everything about us, from our eye or hair colour to the way our bodies grow and develop, including our likelihood of developing certain medical disorders. Genes are arranged inside 23 pairs of **chromosomes** (threadlike structures that are found in every cell in the body). There are millions of different ways that the genes can be arranged on the 46 chromosomes. This makes it difficult to determine which genes might be defective.

One clue came when scientists noticed that almost all people born with **Down's syndrome** develop the 'tangles' and **plaques** in the brain associated with Alzheimer's disease (see pages 6–7). Due to a genetic error, people with Down's syndrome have a third copy of chromosome 21. Experts studied this chromosome and found a defective gene, which allows a build-up of an abnormal **protein**, **beta amyloid**, in the brain. This stops brain cells from working properly (see page 7). Only a small number of people who have the inherited form of early-onset disease have this defective gene.

Other defective genes have been found on chromosomes 1 and 14. If someone with one of these defective genes has children, half of those children will go on to develop Alzheimer's disease in later life. For the average person, however, the chance of developing early-onset disease is only 1 in 1000.

Late-onset disease

No one is sure what causes late-onset disease. Once a person is over the age of 65 the risk of developing Alzheimer's disease increases to about 1 in 30. Some scientists believe that genes may play a part in the development of this condition. On their own, however, it seems unlikely that genes cause late-onset disease. This suggests that the genes only make a person more likely to get the disease. There needs to be something in the environment, such as a toxic substance in their diet, to actually trigger the disease.

Environmental triggers

While defective **genes** may make it more likely for a person to develop Alzheimer's disease later in life, people with these genes do not necessarily go on to have the disease. Scientists believe that a combination of various environmental factors may trigger the condition. A number of theories have been put forward, some of which are listed below.

Auto-immune disease

Auto-immune diseases are disorders in which the body's **immune system**, which normally fights foreign invaders such as bacteria and viruses, starts to attack some of its own cells. Some scientists think that in some older people, changes in the ageing brain cells may cause the immune system to attack the brain, resulting in Alzheimer's disease. An infection or some chemical in the diet may trigger this possible pathway to the disease.

Prion/slow virus theory

Tiny infectious **protein** particles called **prions** have been identified as a cause of some brain disorders that are similar to Alzheimer's disease. Some experts suggest that prions or **slow viruses** (viruses that cause disease many years later) may be a trigger for Alzheimer's disease.

Head injuries

Alzheimer's disease is unusually common in people who have had whiplash injuries to their neck and head. It is not clear how this injury might cause the disease, and it may just be a coincidence that it is more common in people who have had whiplash injuries than in other people. However, the finding that boxers, too, suffer more often than other people from **dementia** suggests that neck and head injuries may trigger the disease.

Boxers have a high risk of suffering head and neck injuries.

Aluminium and mercury

Some small research studies have suggested that aluminium might be directly involved in the development of Alzheimer's disease. However, most experts now believe that this is very unlikely.

Another theory suggested that the mercury used years ago for filling in holes left in teeth after tooth decay might have leaked out and somehow cause Alzheimer's disease. This is now thought to be unlikely but more research is being done.

Reducing the risk

Increasing evidence suggests that what is good for the heart is also good for the brain. Keeping fit and healthy may reduce the risk of developing all forms of dementia. General advice includes:

- Not smoking
- Eating a healthy diet (a diet low in salt and fat, and high in fresh fruit and vegetables) can help reduce blood pressure
- Taking regular exercise
- Having regular blood pressure checks by a GP
- Avoiding head injuries (for example, wearing a helmet for cycling).

How common is Alzheimer's disease?

Alzheimer's disease is very rare in young people but becomes more and more common as people age. Up to the age of 65, only 1 person in 1000 will develop the disease. But in people over the age of 85 it affects one person out of every three.

It can happen to anyone

Anyone can get Alzheimer's disease. Since announcing to the world he had Alzheimer's disease in 1992, former US president, Ronald Reagan and his wife, Nancy, have raised millions of dollars for research into Alzheimer's disease. Other famous people with Alzheimer's disease have helped to raise awareness of the condition.

The life of British novelist, Dame Iris Murdoch, who died in 1999 after a long struggle with Alzheimer's disease, was the subject of the film *Iris*.

Funding research

The research funds and extra publicity attracted through the work of famous people is very welcome. But the governments of every nation in the world have to provide better funding for research into all forms of **dementia** and for better care for the millions of people affected by it. In the UK there

Every little step counts: sponsored walks such as this one in Austin, Texas, USA, raise much-needed money for research into Alzheimer's disease.

are now about three quarters of a million people with dementia – more than 18,000 of them are younger people (under the age of 65). In the USA, about 4 million people have dementia; in Australia about 170,000; and in New Zealand 38,000. Almost two-thirds of these people have Alzheimer's disease.

It is estimated that 66 per cent of all the people in the world with Alzheimer's disease live in developing countries. Yet these countries often lack doctors, nurses, **occupational therapists** and counsellors to help people with the disease and to support those who care for them.

Famous people with Alzheimer's disease

- Rita Hayworth (1918–1987), US film star of over 40 films, including *Only Angels Have Wings* and *Gilda*.
- Charlton Heston (1924–), US film star of such epic movies as *Ben-Hur* and *The Ten Commandments*.
- Iris Murdoch (1919–1999), British novelist and philosopher. Her best-known books include *The Bell* (1958) and *The Sea, the Sea* (1978).
- Ronald Reagan (1911–), former actor and president of the USA (right).

A growing concern

Over the next 25 years the number of people with Alzheimer's disease and other forms of **dementia** is expected to increase dramatically. More people are living past the age of 65, so the chances of developing Alzheimer's disease get higher as people grow older. The second reason is that there was a boom in the number of babies born after the Second World War. In 25 years' time, many of these people will be reaching their 70s and 80s and developing Alzheimer's disease.

It is difficult to work out exactly how many people throughout the world have Alzheimer's disease because not all countries recognize the disease or keep count of how many people develop it. Not everyone will have been specifically diagnosed as having Alzheimer's disease. Some countries only keep count of people with all types of dementia, but we know that more than half of them will have Alzheimer's disease.

Estimating figures

Experts estimate that there are 18 million people with dementia in the world today, of whom more than 9 million have Alzheimer's disease.

By the year 2025, there will be about 34 million people with dementia and by 2050 it is estimated that this number will grow to 70 million. By this time, about 70 per cent of people with dementia will live in developing countries, such as Brazil and India. In the USA, where the elderly population is growing rapidly, it is predicted that the number of people with dementia will grow from 4 million now to 16 million by the year 2050.

Counting the cost

This 'rising tide' of people with dementia will have a huge impact on the many people directly caring for them. Many will have to give up their jobs to look after their loved ones for 24 hours a day. US experts have worked out that it will cost 61,000 million dollars a year – enough to buy 600 trans-Atlantic airliners – to treat and look after all the people in the USA with dementia. Much of this cost will be to cover the lost wages of people who might have to give up their jobs to look after someone with the disease.

"There is an urgent need for more research into the causes, prevention and treatment of this devastating disease."

(Stephen McConnell, President and Chief Executive Officer of the Alzheimer's Association, USA, July 2002)

Early signs and symptoms

It can be difficult to spot the first symptoms of different types of **dementia**. When a grandparent becomes more forgetful, it may just seem to be part of getting older. But when the family look more closely, it is clear that the person is behaving very differently from their normal self.

People in the early stages of Alzheimer's disease may seem more absent minded, misplacing things or repeating themselves. They may sometimes be confused or do odd things such as put the milk in the oven instead of the fridge. However, it is often only when a person has been diagnosed with Alzheimer's disease that close friends and family can look back and realize that the small changes in behaviour were probably the beginning of the condition.

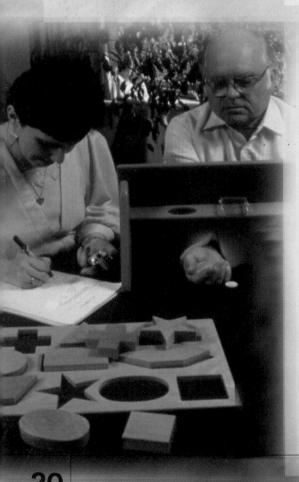

Memory tests

To help make a diagnosis, a doctor may use a simple memory test. This might include asking a few basic questions about recent events and past memories, such as:

- How old are you?
- What is your date of birth?
- What is the day today?
- What month are we in?
- What year is it?
- When was the First World War?
- What is the name of the prime minister or president?
- Where are you now?
- Remember an address, such as '20 Elm Street', and repeat it after five minutes.
- Count backwards from 20 to 1.

This man is taking part in a timed memory test to see if he can remember shapes correctly.

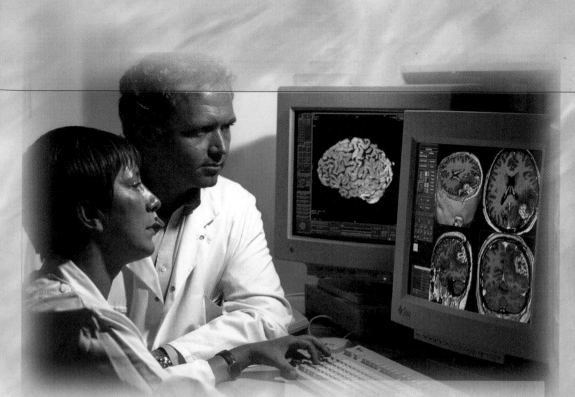

CT scans show pictures of cross sections through the brain.

Making a diagnosis

No single test can show for certain that a person has Alzheimer's disease. But doctors may use brain scans, memory tests and blood tests to rule out other illnesses. This enables them to make a correct diagnosis around 90 per cent of the time.

A brain scan may provide a picture of what changes are taking place in a person's brain. Brain scans can be done in several different ways, including a special type of X-ray technique called **computerized tomography** (a **CT scan**) to show pictures of 'slices' through the brain. Another type of scan is called a **magnetic resonance imaging** scan (**MRI scan**). The MRI scan produces a more detailed image of the brain using radio signals produced by the body in response to the effects of a very strong magnet inside the scanner.

❝I'd check my toothbrush for wetness to see if I'd brushed my teeth, I'd check my towel to see if I'd had my shower.❞

(Marilyn Truscott, a Canadian scientist who was diagnosed with Alzheimer's disease in 1998)

Living with Alzheimer's disease

Everyone who has Alzheimer's disease will experience it in their own way. Generally speaking, the condition can be looked at as a series of stages, where the symptoms gradually become worse over time. However, many of these symptoms may appear earlier or later, or not at all.

Progression of Alzheimer's

Alzheimer's disease usually begins with small changes in a person's behaviour or abilities. A common sign is **short-term memory** loss (other early signs are mentioned on page 20). It is important for carers not to do things for the person that they can manage to do themselves; they will feel better if they can continue to remain independent for as long as they are able. Certain memory skills people learned when they were much younger, such as playing a musical instrument, or swimming the breaststroke, may survive for many years into the illness. This may be because these involve a different type of memory called procedural memory – a 'how to do things' form of memory, which appears to escape damage longer than other memory systems.

During the middle stage, a person with Alzheimer's disease will need more and more support to help them with everyday tasks, such as cooking, eating, washing and going to the toilet. Their memory loss will worsen, and names may become especially hard to remember. Other symptoms include failing to recognize family members, or confusing one person with another. Some people at this stage get more easily upset or angry than they used to. They may become restless and suffer **insomnia** (an inability to sleep). Some people get confused about where they are, or wander off and become lost.

During this stage the person with Alzheimer's disease may put themselves or other people at risk of harm through their forgetfulness. For example, they may switch on a gas cooker and forget to light it, allowing gas to leak out, which could cause an explosion. Damage to the part of the brain responsible for behaviour may cause them to behave inappropriately, such as going outside for a walk in their pyjamas. Some people may even have **hallucinations** (seeing or hearing something that is not really there).

Some people with Alzheimer's disease will need help to get dressed.

"My memory might not be as good as it was, but it doesn't stop me from being me."

(Anonymous person with Alzheimer's disease quoted in the book *Tangles and Starbursts* by Sharon Bailey and Julia Darling)

Living with Alzheimer's disease

Advanced stages

Eventually people with Alzheimer's disease may need constant care throughout the day and night. They may lose their memory completely and not be able to recognize family members. They may become very weak and have some difficulty walking as the part of the brain that controls movements of the muscles becomes damaged by the disease. It is important that anything that might increase their risk of suffering a fall is sorted out – for example, loose doormats, trailing electrical cables, or shoes and other clutter lying around on the floor.

Some people with Alzheimer's become so frail that they have to stay in bed or use a wheelchair. Eating can become very difficult, as they have trouble swallowing food properly, and they are likely to become thinner – though a few eat more and put on weight. At this stage, they may become **incontinent**, which means they lose control of their bladder and they may also lose control of their bowel. Many people remain at home and are cared for by their family throughout the course of their illness. Others eventually go into a nursing home, where nurses and other professional people provide very good full-time care for them. This is often not possible in developing countries where there are few nursing homes.

Once the disease has progressed this far, people tend to talk very little due to the increased damage to the parts of the brain responsible for speech. Sometimes they become restless and seem to be looking for someone or something. They may suddenly become aggressive or very upset, especially if they feel threatened in some way.

Love and reassurance

But although the person now may not even recognize close family members and not seem to understand what anyone says to them, they are still able to respond to kindness and gentleness. It can be reassuring if their hand is held and someone talks to them in a calm soothing voice. Or they may enjoy smelling flowers, scented candles, or listening to music.

People with Alzheimer's disease may become frail during the advanced stages and may find it difficult to walk.

❝My mother's need for love continued until the end. In her last days, as she lay there, she still responded to a gentle massage, soothing music or soft voices.❞

(Jayne, from Alaska, USA, who cared for her mother who had Alzheimer's disease)

DJ's story

Nineteen-year-old DJ Rodie, a student at McGill University, Montreal, Canada, was eight years old when his grandmother, Addie, first began to show symptoms of Alzheimer's disease. Before she was ill, he remembers the great fun they had, talking and joking, when they went to feed the geese in the park. 'She would do anything to make me laugh – even chase a few geese.'

Addie started to have trouble handling everyday tasks, such as driving over to pick up DJ from his music lessons, or going to the supermarket and remembering which foods she needed. She also began to find it hard to do simple sums, which was very surprising because she had worked as an accountant and been very good at arithmetic. Addie began to lose things and get confused: she would go searching through every room in her house looking for her sister – even though her sister lived many miles away, and had not come to visit. It was then, at the age of 71, that Addie was diagnosed with Alzheimer's disease.

DJ's parents soon realized that Addie could no longer live on her own and so they helped her move in with them. After moving in she kept saying she wanted to go home to her mother and father. DJ's mother and father tried to explain to her that her own parents had died. But each day she forgot and she felt the sadness of losing them again. Sometimes the best way round difficult times was to make jokes. DJ's dad would say if Addie's parents were still alive then they owed him 50 years worth of birthday presents!

As the disease developed, Addie could no longer chat to DJ or remember the words of the songs they used to sing together. Addie has now moved into a nursing home where DJ frequently visits her. He says, 'I'm no longer able to have deep conversations with my grandma, but I can definitely still give her a hug – I can still tell her that I love her very much.'

> **❝I know there will come a day when she will no longer be able to recognize me but I believe she'll still be the same loving, caring person that I spent countless hours with.❞**
>
> **(DJ Rodie, McGill University Montreal, Canada, whose grandmother has Alzheimer's)**

Younger people with Alzheimer's disease

Although Alzheimer's disease is much more common in people over the age of 65 than in younger people, it does affect many people in their 40s and 50s. In the UK there are 18,000 people under the age of 65 with **dementia**, in Australia about 7000 and in the USA more than 60,000. Many doctors often do not realize that people this young can develop dementia and so they do not even consider Alzheimer's disease in their diagnosis. It can take years of tests and examinations before the disease is correctly diagnosed.

When someone develops Alzheimer's in their 40s or 50s, the family faces especially difficult challenges.

Sometimes it is a relief for the person with Alzheimer's disease to know what is wrong with them. Later, it is the family that worries more, seeing the person they love change as their illness progresses. The family may also have the pressure of money worries as the person with Alzheimer's disease and their main carer are no longer able to work.

Young families affected by Alzheimer's disease face huge challenges. It can be difficult for children and young adults to face the fact that, just when they feel they need their mother or father most, he or she cannot support them, and instead needs their help.

❝I cannot run away from it. I cannot hide under a stone ... it's there and I've got to deal with it.❞

(Mary, aged 43, from New Zealand, whose husband has Alzheimer's disease)

Mary's story

Mary Reid, from Tauranga, New Zealand, has been looking after her husband, Michael, since he developed Alzheimer's disease. Their three children, Alicia (15), Brendan (13) and Christopher (10), have also been helping to care for Michael, who was only 44 when he was diagnosed. Michael, who worked as a butcher, had been asked to take a week off work because he was acting strangely. At home he was also doing odd things, such as getting up for work at midnight and having a shower, when he did not need to be up until after 5 a.m. 'One night,' Christopher remembers, 'Dad was standing by the pantry and I asked him if I could have a drink. He said, "Where's the pantry?" and he was standing right beside it – that was pretty scary.'

Mary says that the organization Alzheimer's New Zealand has been a great support, talking through problems and encouraging Michael to take part in group activities.

Michael's illness progressed rapidly, and he is now living in a care home, where his family visit him regularly.

Coping with memory loss

One of the biggest problems for people with Alzheimer's disease is losing their **short-term memory**. They may not remember that they have had breakfast, and start to have it all over again. This kind of memory loss can give the person an unsettling sense of losing control. Carers can do a lot to help during the early stages of the illness. It is important for carers to listen to their fears and frustrations, offer reassurance and consider practical ways that might help.

Memory joggers

Some people with early stage Alzheimer's disease find memory joggers, such as 'to do' lists, diaries and clear, written instructions useful. Not being able to remember loved ones' names is often upsetting. A big display board with photos of family and friends with names clearly marked may help.

Keeping to a routine

It is helpful to stick fairly closely to a routine in which daily activities take place at about the same time each day. This makes the person feel less anxious as it is easier for them to remember what usually happens during the day. It also helps if certain food items or other everyday objects are always put back in the same place.

"I remember an ex-Royal Airforce pilot who had Alzheimer's and used to come to our support meetings. He used to sit there hardly saying a word. Then one day we had a slide-show on military aircraft, and up he was, chatting away to the presenter."

(Barrie Randall, team leader of an Alzheimer's Society voluntary support group in Reading, UK)

Memories from the past

One of the first parts of the brain that becomes damaged by Alzheimer's disease is the part that is responsible for forming new memories. However, memories from the distant past remain clear until much later in the course of the illness. It is important to make every effort to share these early memories with the person. While the person is in the early stages of their illness it can be helpful to start a scrapbook all about their life. This should spark quite a few memories from long ago. The scrapbook will also help anyone else who steps in later to care for the person to know more about who they are.

Looking through a photo album together may spark distant memories, untouched by Alzheimer's disease.

Care and support

Because of the progressive nature of the condition, caring for someone with Alzheimer's disease can eventually become a full-time occupation. It might not be quite so difficult at the start of the illness, but as the disease progresses, activities such as going to the toilet, washing, dressing, eating and sleeping become more and more difficult for the person with Alzheimer's disease to manage without help. It is important to allow the person to do what they can for as long as possible. This may mean allowing them to spend much more time getting dressed, for example.

In the early stages of the illness, a carer can often help the person with Alzheimer's disease to stay active.

Everyday activities may be made a little easier to manage when things are always put back in the same place.

ALICE's CLOSET

Carers can ensure they get to meetings at their local Alzheimer's support group to share experiences with other people with the illness. Physical skills, such as riding a bike or playing golf, are not lost as quickly as memory skills, so these pastimes should continue for as long as the person with Alzheimer's disease is able to enjoy them.

Challenging behaviour

Carers need to deal tactfully and respectfully with any situation where the person with Alzheimer's disease refuses to take part in a particular activity, such as having a bath or changing into clean clothes. Some people with Alzheimer's disease may simply not remember why they need to wash, and they may not recognize when their clothes are dirty. Keeping to a routine such as always running the bath just before bedtime can sometimes make things easier.

A person with Alzheimer's disease may behave inappropriately, such as getting undressed at the dinner table. It is important for carers to remember that they have simply become confused about where they are and what time it is.

Being safety conscious

All family members need to help the person with Alzheimer's disease to reduce any risks to their personal safety. For example, they could check to make sure the person did not switch on a gas hob without lighting it or forget to turn off the stove.

"We had taken my Nan out to a posh restaurant. Just as we began to eat our meal, she opened her purse, pulled out a pair of knickers and threw them on the table. We all laughed loudly, including my Nan."

(Sarah, from Berkshire, UK. She helped care for her grandmother, who died aged 71 of Alzheimer's disease)

33

Care and support

A difficult time

Looking after a mother, father or grandparent with Alzheimer's disease can be very demanding. Many carers have a whole range of feelings to cope with. They may feel angry, sad, tired, depressed, fed up, guilty or scared. It is perfectly normal for someone to have any or all of these feelings at different times. It can be easier for people to cope if they can talk about their feelings with other members of the family, a good friend or a healthcare professional such as a counsellor.

Support for carers

Carers are likely to get ill themselves if they try to do everything on their own. They need to seek help from other members of the family, and from professionals such as **social workers**. Social workers can help find someone to look after the person with Alzheimer's disease during the day to give the carer an opportunity to rest.

Social workers may arrange for cooked meals to be delivered to the person's home, to give the main carer a break.

A young carer may find that they fall behind with their homework or are too tired to concentrate at school. The school needs to be told what is happening at home. Teachers can then help, perhaps by sorting out extra time for the young carer to talk to their form tutor, or by finding them a quiet place to do their homework at lunchtime. It is vital that carers take the time to look after themselves by eating properly, by taking exercise, such as going for a swim, and by maintaining other relationships, such as going to the cinema with friends.

Young carers may feel tired or depressed. It usually helps if they find someone to talk to.

Michael's story

Michael, aged 13, from Gisborne, New Zealand, found it very difficult when his grandfather and grandmother, who both had Alzheimer's disease, came to live with him and his parents.

When his grandfather died, Michael's grandmother seemed to take it out on him. 'She got really angry with me, throwing cups of tea at me and telling me to get out of her house,' he says. 'That really upset me. I always try to be respectful and nice to Gran. She doesn't really know what she's saying or doing. When Mum goes out, I give Gran her tea. At first she used to refuse to eat it because I gave it to her, but now she's OK about it. Sometimes at night after Mum's put her to bed she gets up, so I go and get her back to bed.'

Treatment

There are no drugs that can cure Alzheimer's disease, but there are some that can slow down the speed at which people's symptoms get worse. These drugs are **cholinesterase inhibitors**. They stop an important chemical called acetylcholine from being removed from the brain. Acetylcholine is a **neurotransmitter** that helps brain cells to pass messages to one another. Studies have shown that people with Alzheimer's disease do not have enough acetylcholine.

Everyone is different

Cholinesterase inhibitors are not suitable for everyone with Alzheimer's disease. They tend to be prescribed only for early to middle stages of the disease. Medical experts in each country have to agree on rules to determine which people should take them. It may be, for example, that someone's disease has gone so far that the drugs would do them no good. Every person reacts to the drugs in a slightly different way. Some people have a noticeable improvement, while others are not helped at all. But if someone is helped, the beneficial effects usually last for about one year.

Before prescribing drugs, doctors have to think about the possible side effects. The side effects include dizziness, headaches, nausea, vomiting and diarrhoea. Many people will cope with these unwanted side effects, but for others they may be so upsetting that they cancel out any benefits of the drugs. Different people may have different side effects, and they do not last for the same length of time for all that experience them.

A new treatment?

A new type of drug called memantine may be the first drug that can temporarily stop Alzheimer's disease from damaging the brain. It is the first drug that can be taken by people with middle- or late-stage Alzheimer's disease. Scientists need to do more extensive studies to confirm the results found in a small number of people who were given memantine.

A doctor has to assess how the illness is affecting an individual, before deciding which medicine may help.

After taking the drug, people seemed to think a little more clearly and behave more normally. Memantine appears to protect healthy brain cells from being killed by excess amounts of a neurotransmitter called glutamate that leaks out of cells that have been damaged by Alzheimer's disease. Each person responds differently. Some improve, some remain stable, and in other people it has no effect. Side effects include **hallucinations**, dizziness and headaches.

Alternative treatments

There are many non-drug treatments, also called **alternative therapies**, which may be of help in Alzheimer's disease. These approaches cannot cure the illness, but they may relieve some of the symptoms or improve the quality of life for the person with Alzheimer's disease and their family. Alternative therapies should never be used to replace the medicines prescribed by the person's doctor; but they may be useful to take alongside their usual medicine. It is important that the person or their carer checks first with their doctor before trying any alternative therapy, as it may react badly with other medicines they are taking. Some alternative therapies are listed here.

Acupuncture

In this ancient Chinese therapy, very fine needles are pushed in through the skin to bring about healing. It seems that acupuncture could have some benefit in Alzheimer's disease, but more studies are needed.

Herbal remedies

The herbal remedy *Ginkgo biloba*, which comes from the Chinese Ginkgo tree, appears to reverse some of the memory difficulties of Alzheimer's disease. Many studies are being carried out with this herbal treatment, which causes very few unwanted side effects.

Aromatherapy

Aromatherapy is the use of pleasant-smelling oils and plant extracts to help to relax a person, or encourage a feeling of wellbeing. In Alzheimer's disease, aromatherapy may also have more specific benefits. Research has shown that aromatherapy using the scent of the lemon balm plant may help prevent the loss of the neurotransmitter acetylcholine – one of the key chemicals that allows brain cells to communicate with each other.

Massage

A body massage (right) helps to relax tense muscles and improve blood circulation. Studies have shown that a combination of aromatherapy and massage has helped people with Alzheimer's disease or other types of **dementia** to relax.

Below: People with Alzheimer's disease may find that exercising in water helps them to stay active.

Creative therapies

Many people with Alzheimer's disease find creative therapies such as music, dance, art and gardening stimulating and enjoyable. These activities help people express themselves and make more sense of their environment. Music therapy, in which people come together to make music with the help of a music therapist, seems to improve the symptoms of Alzheimer's disease. Many people also enjoy listening to music or singing or dancing along to their favourite songs.

Reminiscence therapy

Psychological therapies, such as **reminiscence therapy**, can be helpful to some patients with Alzheimer's disease. In reminiscence therapy, the person is shown photographs or films, perhaps of trams, aeroplanes or film stars from their youth. This often brings back many memories. Copies of old adverts for breakfast cereals, tins of beans and other foods can be used to make modern packets and tins look like they did when the person was at school or in their first job. Some carers have borrowed dresses, suits and other clothes that were fashionable when the person was young from local theatre groups to help encourage memories of enjoyable nights out with friends at dances and parties.

Therapists usually provide reminiscence therapy to small groups of people with Alzheimer's disease. By sharing their memories with the group, they can feel proud about their achievements, make new friends and feel less lonely. Reminiscence therapy can be good for carers, too, as they get to know more about their loved one, and learn things from them that helps to increase their respect for the person and understand them more. The aim of this therapy is to emphasize what they can remember, rather than what they have forgotten.

Many local branches of Alzheimer's support groups throughout the world have collections of photos, videotapes and other objects that may be helpful for reminiscence therapy.

Aids for reminiscence therapy

There are many items that may be useful in a session of reminiscence therapy. These include:

- CDs and records from the person's past
- audiotapes of old radio programmes
- videotapes and films of old movies and family events, such as weddings or parties
- photo albums
- fashionable clothes from the person's youth
- souvenirs of important personal events, such as competition trophies or war medals
- old cooking recipes and mock-ups of old tins and food packets.

People to talk to

Alzheimer's disease affects the whole family. So it is important for everyone to talk to one another, share feelings and be supportive. But sometimes help is needed from healthcare professionals with special skills and training, whose job involves working with families affected by Alzheimer's disease. These include **social workers**, community nurses, counsellors, and family doctors.

Voluntary organizations such as the UK Alzheimer's Society and Alzheimer's Australia provide booklets and factsheets about Alzheimer's disease. For people who want to find out more, local groups hold regular meetings for people with Alzheimer's disease and for carers so they can share experiences and offer each other support.

"When someone feels that they have a better understanding of the illness and are not so fearful, then I feel I have made some difference."

(Anne Deck, Counsellor, Alzheimer's Australia)

Helplines

Many organizations operate telephone lines to provide information and support regarding any aspect of Alzheimer's disease. (See pages 52–53 for further details.) Many organizations have local groups run by volunteers. These offer advice and assistance, and usually hold regular meetings during which people with Alzheimer's disease and their carers can meet, share experiences and offer each other support.

Listening to others with similar problems and sharing experiences with people that understand can be very uplifting.

Alzheimer's associations around the world provide practical and emotional help and information to families affected by the disease. They also put pressure on governments to spend more money on services to help look after people with Alzheimer's disease.

Religious leaders

If the person with Alzheimer's or their carer has religious faith, they may find it helpful or comforting to talk to a priest, minister, rabbi or other spiritual leader. It may be helpful and calming for the person to continue to attend religious services. If this is no longer possible, it may be possible for carers to make arrangements for their spiritual leader to visit them at home.

Help on the web

Most national Alzheimer's support organizations have websites, which offer the latest research news and information about the disease. Many have a message board where people with Alzheimer's disease can communicate with others around the world. Carers can also share their experiences with other carers. The websites give addresses and telephone numbers for all local voluntary support groups and services.

Professional care

While some people with Alzheimer's disease will be looked after at home throughout their illness, others will eventually move into a care home. The need for 24-hour care every day can become too much for their family to cope with.

A difficult decision

Moving a mother or father or any other loved one out of their own home into a care home is a difficult thing for any family to do. Sons and daughters may feel that they have let the person down, or worry that the person will not get the same loving care they got at home. By finding out about all the available options, and visiting a number of different homes, the family can choose the best possible care for their relative.

Different types of home

The main difference between a residential home and a nursing home is that the nursing home has trained nurses who can provide nursing care for people with Alzheimer's disease at any time of the day or night. Both types of home will help the person with dressing, washing and going to the toilet, and will give them meals, and take them on walks.

Choosing a home

It is important to find the right kind of care home for the person with Alzheimer's disease. It has to be in a place that is easy for family and friends to visit, and that feels friendly and welcoming. The family will want

to find a place where people are gently encouraged to take part in activities, such as exercising to music, singing, or chatting.

Many carers look for a home in which there is enough room for everyone to sit together during the day if they want to, and which has a safe garden for people to sit in or go for walks in.

By talking to other people living in a nursing home, the family can find one that will suit their loved one. Some people will want a place where they have their own bedroom; they might also like to have their favourite chair or other furniture. The nursing home manager can let the family know if furniture and other personal things can be brought into the home. Regular visits by the family will help the person to settle into a good care home.

Legal matters

It is important that the person with Alzheimer's disease and their family sort out important legal matters while the person is still able to do so. For example, they will need to prepare for a time in their illness when they will no longer be able to pay their own bills and manage their money. The person may also wish to consider what forms of treatment they would or would not like to have later in their illness, when they may be too confused to understand the options available to them.

Enduring power of attorney

An **Enduring Power of Attorney (EPA)** is a legal document with which one person gives one or more people (the attorneys) the power to manage their money and property. The person with Alzheimer's disease (or other forms of **dementia**) can choose for this to happen while they are mentally capable of understanding what they are doing, or they may choose for EPA to come into effect only when they are mentally incapable.

The process of setting up an EPA is complicated and usually requires the help of a legal expert. Because this is a legal document, it must be set up while the person is aware of what is involved and can show that they understand the process. For this reason, it must be done while the symptoms of the disease are still mild.

It is important for a person with Alzheimer's disease to seek legal advice before the illness progresses.

Living wills

A **living will** is a legal document that allows people to state what forms of treatment they would or would not like to have in the future. A living will only concerns a person's medical treatment and has nothing to do with an ordinary will, which states what is to happen to a person's money and property after their death. The person's doctor will keep a copy of the will with their medical records to ensure their instructions are followed. An example of the kind of instruction the person may make in their living will might be that they are to be given no special medical procedure or treatment aimed at prolonging their life.

Different countries have different laws regarding living wills, and changes continue to be made. In the UK, Canada and many states in the USA and Australia, living wills are legally binding: doctors have to follow their instructions or break the law.

How can modern science help?

New drugs that promise to slow down the progression of Alzheimer's disease, and to lessen memory loss and other symptoms are currently being researched. But no cure for the disease looks likely to be discovered in the near future. The Human Genome Project, an international study to identify every single **gene** in the human body, will help in the understanding of how faulty genes cause Alzheimer's disease. It may then be possible using **gene therapy** techniques to repair these genes and prevent Alzheimer's disease from developing. However, this research is still at an early stage and it will be many years before we know how effective gene therapy may be.

Researchers are trying to transplant stem cells into the brain in the hope that these will transform into brain cells and replace those lost due to Alzheimer's disease.

Stem cell transplants

Another possible area of research involves **stem cells**. These are special cells, found in bone marrow and other organs, which can develop into a wide range of different types of cell such as liver or stomach cells. In studies with mice, research has shown that stem cells from the bone marrow transplanted into the heart will change into heart muscle cells, for example. Scientists are now studying the possibility that stem cells transplanted into the brain of a person with Alzheimer's disease may develop into brain cells that might replace those lost due to the disease.

Vitamin therapy

Another area of research covers studies into giving people extra vitamin E and C. It is thought that these may be able to help protect the brain from some of the damage caused by Alzheimer's disease.

Stem cells seen under a powerful microscope.

Stem cell research

Scientists in Melbourne, Australia recently discovered that the brain contains stem cells. Experts had always thought that once nerve cells died they could not be replaced. But the discovery of stem cells suggests that dead nerve cells can be replaced. Why then can the brain not heal itself when damaged by diseases like Alzheimer's? It could be that it is unable to grow new nerve cells fast enough to repair the damage. Scientists are developing new drugs that could increase the rate at which stem cells can transform into nerve cells. This could lead to big improvements in the quality of life of people with Alzheimer's disease.

Looking to the future

People are living longer than ever before and older people are becoming a larger proportion of the population. As the population of older people grows, so does the number of people affected by Alzheimer's disease. Many people throughout the world are now full-time carers for people with the disease.

More training for carers

As well as dealing with the effects of the condition, people with Alzheimer's disease and their families often have expensive bills to pay for medical tests, treatments, and nursing home costs. Carers should be given information about the disease and training to help them look after someone with the disease. A study from Australia has shown that people who receive such training and information do a better job and suffer less stress.

Raising public awareness

The world community needs to ensure that it takes account of the needs of people with Alzheimer's disease and their families, and to help them to live as fulfilling a life as possible. More activities in schools are needed to help young people to understand the disease.

Improving funding and information

The particular problems posed by Alzheimer's disease in the developing world must not be forgotten. It is estimated that by 2050, 70 per cent of all people in the world with Alzheimer's disease will live in developing countries. These countries will need financial help and knowledge from wealthier countries to ease the enormous suffering the disease will cause. The challenge facing every nation now is to ensure they are ready to help the growing number of people affected by Alzheimer's disease.

❝Everybody whose life is affected by [dementia] will find it easier to be courageous [...] when they know the people around them and their government recognize its appalling nature.❞

(Dr Nori Graham, chairman of Alzheimer's Disease International, speaking at the launch of Alzheimer's World Health Day, in April 2001)

Understanding dementia

In 2002 a successful project called 'Dementia on Stage' targeted fifteen- to seventeen-year-old school students in Western Australia. They were given information about dementia and asked to write pieces of drama for a performance on the stage. A series of sketches called *Alzheimer's Anonymous* was one of the award-winning pieces of drama. Understanding of the issues of dementia greatly increased among students after this project.

Information and advice

The following organizations, websites and books can provide a wide range of useful information about Alzheimer's disease and sources of practical support for families affected by this illness.

Contacts in the UK

Alzheimer Scotland
Tel: 0131 243 1453
Fax: 0131 243 1450
24 hour Helpline: 0808 808 3000
Website: www.alzscot.org
Provides information, support and local services throughout Scotland for people with dementia, and their carers.

Alzheimer's Society
Tel: 020 7306 0606   Fax: 020 7306 0808
Helpline: 0845 300 0336
(8.30 a.m. – 6.30 p.m. Monday to Friday)
Email: info@alzheimers.org.uk
Website: www.alzheimers.org.uk
This organization is the main charity in the UK for people suffering from any form of dementia and their carers. The website provides a wealth of information on all aspects of the disease, and has links to over 70 local branches of the organization throughout the UK.

MIND
Tel. 020 8519 2122
Fax: 020 8522 1725
Website: www.mind.org.uk
This large charity works for carers and people suffering from mental health problems. The website contains dozens of useful booklets on various illnesses, including one on dementia.

Contacts in Ireland

Alzheimer Society of Ireland
Tel: 01 2846616
Fax: 01 2846030
Free Helpline: 1800 341 341
Website: www.alzheimer.ie
The leading dementia care organization in Ireland, with 29 branches across the country.

Contacts in the USA

The Alzheimer's Association
Helpline: 800-272-3900
Tel: 1-312-335-8700
Fax: 1-312-335.1110
Website: www.alz.org
This is the largest national voluntary organization and the top private funder of research into the causes, treatment and prevention of Alzheimer's disease. A wide range of information is available on the website, which has a message board, poetry corner and gallery of artwork.

Alzheimer's Disease Education and Referral Center
Website: www.alzheimers.org/
Provides detailed information about Alzheimer's disease and the latest research.

Contacts in Canada

Alzheimer Society
Tel: (416) 488-8772
Fax: (416) 488-3778
Free Helpline: 1-800-616-8816
Website: www.alzheimer.ca
As well as providing a wide range of information, this society has a busy website message board which has a section posting creative writing from people with Alzheimer's disease and their carers.

Contacts in Australia

Alzheimer's Australia
Tel: (02) 6254 4233
Fax: (02) 6278 7225
24-hour Helpline: 1800 639 331
Website: www.alzheimers.org.au
Alzheimer's Australia provides information and support across the country, coordinated by eight regional offices. Fact sheets are available in Greek, Italian, Polish, Arabic, Vietnamese and Chinese languages.

Contacts in New Zealand

Alzheimer's New Zealand
Tel: 03 365 1590
Fax: 03 379 8744
Free Helpline: 0800 004 001
Website: www.alzheimers.org.nz
This national charity coordinates the support services and fundraising activities of 22 member organizations. Among the services provided are carer education programmes and day care.

International contacts

Alzheimer's Disease International
Tel: +44 20 7620 3011
Fax: +44 20 7401 7351
Website: www.alz.co.uk
This organization is an umbrella group of 64 Alzheimer associations throughout the world. It provides information and funds research, including programmes to improve the care of people with Alzheimer's disease in developing countries.

Further Reading

The Long and Lonely Road: Insights Into Living with Younger Onset Dementia, Alzheimer's Australia, 2003

The Milk's in the Oven, by Lizi Hann; Mental Health Foundation, 1998

Tangles and Starbursts: Living with Dementia, by Julia Darling and Sharon Bailey; Alzheimer's Society UK, North Tyneside Branch, 2001

Understanding Dementia: a Guide for Young Carers, Health Education Board for Scotland, 1996

All the King's Horses, by Laura C. Stevenson; Corgi Books, 2001
A sensitive fictional adventure story of a young brother and sister trying to help their Grandfather, a former racehorse trainer, who has dementia.

Glossary

Age of Enlightenment
the name for a period in the 18th century when leading thinkers encouraged people to use their own logic to understand the world rather than follow traditional beliefs

alternative therapies
various treatments that people may find helpful in addition to the traditional medical treatments used by doctors

asylum
a place where mentally ill people were kept. Although they were meant to be places of shelter and support, they were often overcrowded and made a person's illness worse.

auto-immune disease
when the body's immune system mistakenly attacks its own cells

beta amyloid
an abnormal protein found in clumps throughout the brain in Alzheimer's disease. It is thought to block normal communication between nerve cells.

cholinesterase inhibitors
dementia drugs that stop the breakdown of acetylcholine, the chemical that transmits messages between brain nerve cells

chromosome
thread-like structure inside cells, which carries the genes

Creutzfeldt-Jacob disease (CJD)
a rare form of dementia caused by an infectious agent called a prion

CT (computerised tomography) scan
an X-ray scan that results in a series of pictures of 'slices' through the brain or other organs

dementia
incurable loss of brain function, involving memory, thinking and concentraton. It is caused by injury or brain diseases, such as Alzheimer's disease.

depression
a mental disorder characterized by feeling extremely gloomy, inadequate and being unable to concentrate. It is quite different from feeling a little down in spirits, or having the temporary 'blues'.

Down's syndrome
a genetic condition in which the person affected is born with an extra chromosome, and has various physical problems and a learning disability

early-onset disease
Alzheimer's disease that develops in people younger than 65

Enduring Power of Attorney (EPA)
a legal document with which one person gives one or more people (the attorneys) the power to manage their money and property

frontal lobes
the parts of the brain lying just behind the forehead, which are responsible for planning, behaviour and personality

gene
information within body cells that determines a person's characteristics, for example hair colour or nose shape. Genes are passed down to us by our parents.

gene therapy
a technique in which normal genes are inserted into cells in place of missing or faulty genes to correct genetic disorders

hallucinations
seeing or hearing things that are not really there

immune system
the body's natural defence against disease and infection

incontinent
loss of the ability to control the bladder or the bowels

insomnia
inability to sleep

living will
a written statement explaining how a person should be treated medically when they are no longer able to make such decisions themselves

MRI (magnetic resonance imaging) scan
a type of scan that produces pictures of body organs using a powerful magnet

neurologist
a scientist that specializes in disorders of the brain and nervous system

neurotransmitters
chemicals that act as 'messengers' between the nerve cells of the brain

occupational therapist
a person who can advise on ways of helping someone to maintain their living skills and look after themselves

Pick's disease
a rare form of dementia that affects language skills, personality and memory

plaques
layers of an abnormal form of the protein beta-amyloid, which form in areas between brain cells

prion
an infectious protein particle. Studies suggest it is the cause of Creutzfeldt-Jacob disease and similar illnesses.

protein
a compound containing nitrogen, which is an essential part of body tissues such as muscle

reminiscence therapy
a treatment that aims to stimulate people's memories by showing objects they would have seen in their past

short-term memory
the type of memory we use to remember a shopping list. Short-term memories tend to be lost in a matter of hours.

slow virus
a virus that causes disease many years after infection

social worker
a professional who can offer advice on matters to do with money, day care and accommodation

stem cell
a stem cell is a cell that can become virtually any type of cell in the body

tangles
in Alzheimer's disease, these are groups of twisted fine fibres of an abnormal form of a protein called tau, which builds up inside brain cells causing them to burst and die

tau
a protein that is essential to support the structure of cells and to transport materials from one part of the cell to another

Index